P9-DGL-226

# Striper Chronicles

## East Coast Surf Fishing Legends & Adventures

Leo N. Orsi, Jr.

Striper Chronicles Web Site: Http://www.striperchronicles.com

Cover photo courtesy Malcolm Greenaway
Photo page 66 courtesy Lou Feierabend
Color conté page 70 courtesy Evelyn Rhodes
Photos page 78 & 79 courtesy Mickey and Richard Colasanto
Photo page 83 courtesy John Swienton
Photos page 112 &113 courtesy John Grant
Photo page 124 courtesy Joe Szabo
All other photos by the author

Jacket design by Cathi Stevenson
Striped bass and Mirrolure illustrations by Samantha Wall

**Library of Congress Cataloging-in-Publication Data**

**Library of Congress Control Number: 2003097385**

Orsi, Leo, N., Jr.

Striper Chronicles / by Leo N. Orsi, Jr.

**ISBN** 0-9745952-9-2

Manufactured in the United States of America
First Edition / Second Printing

***This book is dedicated to my darling daughter, Kristen, who left us on June 26, 2002, to fish in God's ocean alongside my father. Lovingly and appropriately nicknamed "Sweetness" by her Nana, she had a beautiful heart and a loving way with all of God's creatures — every creature she touched seemed to somehow know and understand her. She was a champion — forever remembered and forever missed.***

# Contents

# Foreword

**F**or many of us, any book on the striper surf is welcome. One reason for this is the paucity of solid literature on an exciting and rewarding endeavor such as heaving a lure into a hostile sea without knowing if one is fishing wrong in a mother-lode of stripers or right on a barren shore. Thus, adventure lies in the fore of every surfcaster who has ever wondered about his methods and surfcasting spots and how they will come together.

The striped bass is the most popular marine species in the Northwest Atlantic, and the set for Leo Orsi's play is smack dab in the middle of that species' range. How far wrong can a surfcasting book go when it is focused on two of the most productive shore fishing grounds on our coast — Jamestown and Block Island? Both places have provided me with memorable surfcasting during a time that I probably will never see again. In his own recollection of these places and how they played out for him, Orsi skillfully takes us back to shores that are known and loved by many and to a life I, too, once knew and loved.

There ought to be a saying among fishing writers that being a historian is the writer's last assignment. No one is ever entrusted with that job until his hair has grayed and his memorable fishing yarns have fermented. Although I don't want that billet, there seems to be few left who can do it. Moreover, I can tell you some pretty good stories about both Block Island and Jamestown — two locations that have danced in my dreams as much as any during my lifetime adventures in surfcasting. In 1969 our son, Dick, and I took the ferry out of Galilee for "the Block" to investigate the monster bluefish we had been hearing about from boatmen friends. Then, bluefish were much more rare than they are today; truly, they were considered to be almost an exotic species. We were successful with the choppers but, inasmuch as we were devoted surfcasters, we could not allow the night surf of Mohegan Bluffs to go untested. To our astonishment, decent stripers were in the same surf after dark in midsummer. It was a great experience for an aspiring writer like the Frank Daignault of that time, who was then 34 years old, and it formed the basis for my first published article in 1970 for *Salt Water Sportsman* called "Block Island Safari."

How many times have you heard *if I knew then what I know now*? That notion haunts me every time I think of the moby stripers that seemed to circle Jamestown, again around the same time, back in the early '70s. If only we had had the presence of mind to associate the fish we were catching nightly from the Jamestown Bridge with what had to be off of Jamestown's rocks.

What a job we could have done on nights when the moon shone too brightly or when the tide was wrong for the bridge. Orsi does more than expose the great fishing of the time. He also examines the influence of surfcasting's drama upon those who dabble in its craft while risking a greater commitment. I see, between the lines of these pages, that we had to have been ethereal shadows of the time passing in the night. His references to Rebelle Felice clinch that notion. Not only did my wife, Joyce, and I benefit from Felice's generosity, but we later came to know his high-liner brothers, Pergo and Eddie, on the distant beaches of Cape Cod.

There is charm in the good old days of striper fishing. Indeed, new striper stories are a lot like wine in that they benefit from sitting a while and fermenting. The Chronicles seizes upon that. The "googan" quality of every novice hides beneath the skin of all of us because nobody is born knowing how to surf cast. Thus, there is humor in the author's examination of the beginner. Orsi has captured that while developing the character in both himself and his friends. Still, the lead player in this striper book is the lineside herself.

Who among us has not languished on the shores of the striper coast, involved in a love affair of surfcasting for striped bass? Who among us has not risen from his bed, wide-eyed in the deep night, terrified at the notion that somewhere other surfmen were doing it without him? Which of you has not snubbed down on a drag, or pulled too hard, or failed to moisten a knot amid the fits of apprehension of a wildly running lineside? Indeed, our mistakes, our dreams, our misadventures, are universal to the shore fisher's plight. Nevertheless, there is pleasure in validating your own experiences in the pages of another surfman's book. Most of all, we never see enough of the squid stink and salt spray of the written surfcasting you will see here — and you can't have too much of that. Cinch a surf belt around your oilskins and plot a course for Block Island or Jamestown.

Frank Daignault

# Acknowledgements

Without the assistance and encouragement of many of my friends and other industry professionals, the writing of the Chronicles would never have been possible. There were so many people involved in my surfcasting journey of over 30 years and they all contributed in one way or another to the experiences and stories that are written here. To all of them that you will read about in the pages that follow, my hat is off in gratitude. It is also necessary and appropriate that I mention the names of a few friends and acquaintances who made special contributions to the composition of the Chronicles either through their generosity or their active participation, or both. First and foremost in this category are my two best and lifelong friends, Raymond Pettus and Bruce Shepley. Together with these two, I have had the opportunity to experience some of the most enjoyable moments of my life, regardless of whether the fish were biting. The sub-stage or the home base for the Chronicles was graciously provided by Bill and Mary Shepley, and Harvey and Susan Waxman. Year after year, these couples have generously welcomed me and other members of the Princeton Fishing Team into their island homes, continuously making us all feel like we were part of their families. A huge thank-you also goes to Susan Feldman for taking the time away from her busy schedule at Putnam to copy edit the Chronicles — her assistance and advice were invaluable as was that of Jennifer Johnson, who also contributed editorial advice and assistance. And while on the subject of invaluable contributions, a special mention of gratitude must be given to Frank Daignault for his many contributions to this book and also for the inspiration he provided through his own surf fishing stories and adventures contained in at least six books that he has written on the subject. No book of this nature would be complete without pictures and artwork, and because of the generosity of two of New England's finest professionals, Malcolm Greenaway (the book's cover photo) and Evelyn Rhodes (the Creek Bait Shop crayon conté), the book is beautifully enhanced by their marvelous talents. Many thanks also to Mickey and Richard Colasanto and John Swienton for their recounts of two great island fathers: Rebelle Felice and Mac Swienton. And to NBC News anchor Brian Williams, for taking time from his enormously busy schedule to contribute some insightful reflections on his relationship with Mac Swienton. Likewise, special mention and thanks are extended to publisher Bruce Montgomery and editor-at-large

Kevin Weaver, both of the Block Island Times, for their contribution of excerpts of an exceptional Times article. And finally, a particular mention of thanks to the "seasoned salts" like Charley Soares, Joe Mollica, John Martini, Joe Szabo, John Grant and Steve Smith — all of whom enthusiastically contributed stories, memories and viewpoints of their own chronicles — how easy and enjoyable it was to chat with all of them about the lore of the sea, the lore of the striper, and the lore of the islands.

# Preface

I often said that one day I would write a book about the magnificent adventures that I have been so fortunate to experience in over 30 years of fishing for the ever-intriguing striped bass — adventures exceeded in merit only by the incredible friends that I have made and the people that I have met along the way. The friends and people, a fabulous array and a wide spectrum of endearing and charismatic surf fishing personalities, are what make the adventures that are chronicled throughout this book so very special and so uniquely interesting. However, as differing as the personality spectrum may be, there are two basic commonalities: a deep appreciation for the sport of striped bass fishing and a love for two of the most spectacular islands on earth — Jamestown and the Block. From my early years as a child, listening to stories told by my father about pursuing the mystical striped fish in the great surf, to experiencing one of history's greatest Block Island striper blitzes with two of my very best friends, the following chapters will take you on a journey of striped bass fishing adventures that were tremendously exciting, almost always challenging and sometimes just plain comical. But just as the tide will always raise the level of the sea, it must always take some of its waters back, and so too, along with a plethora of enjoyable fishing experiences also came tragedy. The rocky coastlines of Jamestown and Block Island are punishing and dangerous environments when the ocean becomes enraged — God help the fisherman who loses sight of the power and the fury of the sea.

Above all, the purpose of this book is not to instruct others in the methods or techniques of fishing for striped bass. There are so many great "how to" books on the market these days and most of them are devoted primarily and comprehensively to cataloging the proper approach to pursuing and catching striped bass. This is not a "how to" book. This is a book about "how it went" for over 30 years of fishing for stripers. And sometimes it went well — exciting catches of very large fish in historic proportions, pleasant fishing conditions and mild surf. Sometimes it was simply ruining a perfectly good day by trying to fish; and sometimes, well, the intentions were genuine, but the results were nothing more than amusing fishing stories best suited for fireplace lamentation. The expert surfcaster as well the beginner (and even the non-fisherman) will relate to and appreciate the unsuspected variety of situations that evolve around the basic and relatively simple plan of all surf fishing expeditions — to catch fish, lots of them. But now and then the forces of nature, Murphy's Law of Fishing, and luck (or the lack thereof) have different agendas for the unsuspecting fisherman. Hurricanes, dense fog, equipment failures, pitch-black nights and The Perfect Storm — all contribute to some wild and exciting fishing stories.

A better stage for the chronicles you are about to read could not be envisioned on any other island pair than Jamestown and the Block. These two islands are abundantly rich in fishing legends, fishing lore and fishing history — particularly as it relates to the striped bass. It was no secret, even several hundred years ago, that each island had a plentiful supply of the striped fish swimming throughout its waters. Anglers in the mid- to late 1800s had already discovered the great fishing opportunities that existed around these islands, and some anglers were so enthusiastic about the sport that they went through the painstaking process of drilling iron pipes into the surf's boulders in order to erect bass stands from which they could fish for the linesiders. To this day, hundreds of trophy stripers have been taken by Jamestown surfcasters, and the largest striped bass ever taken by a rod-and-reel angler was reported to have been caught by a Block Island surf fisherman in 1887 (over 85 pounds!). Unfortunately, the catch was never officially certified and as such, is not recognized as the world record today. In fact, what turned my attention to the Block as a young URI grad student were the reports coming from the island during the late '70s of very large bass that were consistently being caught from its shores while the rest of New England (except for a few places on the Cape) was suffering from a severe decline in the overall bass population. During those years, almost all the bass that were caught on Block Island were big fish and those fishermen who knew about the island's secret did their best to try to keep it quiet. Discovering the two islands and their fishing secrets along with my two lifelong high school friends was an adventure extraordinaire. In the pages that follow, I have captured many of the challenges we encountered as young, aspiring fishermen and the pathway, albeit sometimes rocky, that we followed throughout the years on our way to becoming knowledgeable and accomplished surfcasters. Equally as interesting and entertaining was the cast of friends and characters we met along the journey — none more spectacular in his manner and in his passion for striped bass fishing than the late Rebelle Felice, the past owner of the Jamestown Creek Bait Shop. Rebelle was a father of the island, a monarch and protector of its environment, and for two teenage striped bass fishermen wannabees, he was an eyeful *and* an earful. For new Jamestown fishermen, he was your initiation into the island's sport fishing scene — and if you never had the opportunity to know him, the accounts in these pages will give you a pleasurable and entertaining insight into an island legend. Another legend, equally as charismatic and passionate about striped bass fishing and the marine environment, was the late Mac Swienton, owner and proprietor of Twin Maples Cottages and Bait Shop on the Block. Mac was another island father and a monarch of its waters — he was an inspiration to his island community and to the fishermen he counseled in every subject from equipment repairs to world affairs. If you never knew Mac, you will enjoy reading about his life and exuberant spirit, and if you did know him, you will smile remembering his character through these pages.

While there is certainly no substitute for actually being on one of the islands with your surf rod in hand, casting into the sea, sometimes curling up in front of the fireplace on a cold night with a wee nip and a great book can bring you close. Here are some adventures that may bring you home again or that may entice you to try a magnificent sport if you have never before done so.

**Leo N. Orsi, Sr., with a Jersey shore striper, 1954.**

**The author, Leo Jr., and Dad — the inspiration of a young surfcaster-to-be.**

# Chapter I

## Father's Passions, a Lifelong Friend and Two Islands

It started about 48 years ago. I was 3 years old then and we lived in Princeton, New Jersey. My mother took a picture of me standing next to my father and a 10-pound striper that he had caught at the Jersey shore the previous evening. The fish was nearly as big as I was. My father was as passionate about striper fishing as he was about almost anything else in life. His stories about the great striped fish that possessed incredible fighting power and an uncanny level of intelligence were like listening to fairy tales of men battling mythical sea creatures. For if a man was fortunate enough to have successfully captured the great striper, he was to be held in high esteem as a skillful and accomplished fisherman — one who battled the perils of the night and the raging surf (not to mention the elements) and hence outsmarted the cagey fish in its own environment. Even more alluring to a youngster was the fact that at age 3, and for many years to follow, I was told that I was too young to fish for stripers at night. It was simply too dangerous.

My father liked to fish from the rock jetties along the New Jersey oceanfront, and exclusively at night. Between the extremely slippery, slime-covered jetty rocks and the ocean breakers pounding at the jetty sides, he was quite correct — it was no place for a small child. Nevertheless, the stories that came back from each night's excursions were enchanting. They always seemed to have a mysterious element and only served to heighten my desire to one day be able to accompany my father.

That day (night, actually) finally came, although in fairness to my father, prior to my first night of bass fishing we had taken frequent trips to the New Jersey shore to fish during the day from the beaches. It was great fun, but it took place during the day and we never caught any stripers. During the mid-'50s and early '60s, the Jersey shore was loaded with another, much smaller, fish — the blowfish. You could sometimes catch over 100 in a day, and since the stripers never seemed to be around during the daytime, catching blowfish was fishing action and the whole family loved it. The blowfish is excellent table fare as well. In fact, I think it was the only fish (aside from Mrs. Paul's fish sticks) that my sisters and I would eat at that age. Many other anglers had also discovered this delectable little fish and as a consequence, the number of blowfish declined to almost extinction over the following years.

When I had reached the age of 12, my father finally decided that it was time to introduce me to jetty fishing at night for the elusive and powerful striper — not, of course, without considerable whining and prodding from me. It was a fishing experience that I have never forgotten. To finally be able to experience this mystical piscatorial challenge was almost more than I could stand. My father liked to bottom-fish for stripers using large chunks of squid as bait. He would sometimes rig an entire 10- to 12-inch squid on what seemed to me at the time to be an enormous hook. After all, I was used to tiny blowfish hooks.

So off to the Jersey shore we went; Manasquan Inlet to be exact. The fishing that night was slow. We had caught a few small skates which broke the lull, but not much except the crabs was taking the squid bait. We used Penn conventional reels in the ’50s and ’60s, spooled with 50-pound test nylon braided line. And the way jetty fishing worked was that one would cast out a large piece of squid, if not the whole squid itself, rigged to a 50-pound test monofilament leader and a 4-ounce pyramid sinker, all linked together by a three-way swivel. This is still a remarkably effective method for catching stripers and it's a method used even today in New England by many "chunkers," as they're called.

My father liked to hold his fishing rod instead of putting it in a sand spike with a loose drag. That way, he claimed, you could set the hook before the fish discovered that there was something unusual going on — as he told me over and over again, these fish are very smart. Well, it didn't quite happen that way during my first jetty trip with him. Even at the ripe old age of 12, kids have a tendency to get bored when the fishing action slows, and that night, the action started out slow and tapered off from there. Realizing this, I decided that I would go over to the makeshift cutting board that my father had set up on a rock and cut some of the squid into strips as I had seen him do earlier. I guess I was just trying to feel important and look as if I knew what I was doing in front of the other fishermen who were also out on the rocks that evening. Upon seeing this, and also seeing that I was making a miserable mess out of some perfectly fine squid baits, my father put down his rod to come and take over the process. I don't think that his rod was down for more than 15 seconds before we both heard the clacking of the rod and reel against the rocks as it was pulled off the jetty and into the water. We turned around just in time to see it go off the side of the last rock and into the ocean. Oddly enough, when we ran over to the side of the jetty to see what we could see, upon shining his flashlight down into the water, my father discovered that the rod, still attached to the fish, was lying motionless on some rocks under about five feet of water. "There it is! There it is!" I remember him shouting. "I'm going in after it. I can get it!" he said as he motioned me out of his way and started to remove his shoes and clothes. But remembering all the previous cautions that I had received about the dangerous waves and the perils of the slippery rocks, I frantically pleaded with him not to go into the water and down onto the rocks — almost to the point of tears. All the while, both of us had our eyes glued to the submerged rod, and by this time the other fishermen had come over to see what all the commotion was about. Somehow, sanity prevailed, and we just watched as what seemed to take an eternity actually happened in less than a few minutes. Then, suddenly, the rod swiftly and silently slid away into the ocean depths with its pilot never to be discovered.

A giant bass? A shark? Perhaps a large skate? I can tell you that my father knew what it was, and with disgusted certainty. It was the biggest bass he'd ever hooked! According to his assessment, it would have taken at least the two of us just to get it to the car...... well, he got more mileage out of this "one that got away" than if he had landed it. My punishment was that I had to hear that story a million times — and now you know it too.

My father's name was Leo also (Leo N. Orsi, Sr.). He was a striper legend, right down to the pipe that you used to see so many of the other old-time fishermen position just off to the side of the mouth while having their pictures taken with the day's catch — sort of like scotch and cigars today, I guess. His love for striper fishing and his respect for the striped bass as the "king of the surf" were infectious. I owe my introduction to this great sport to him and, after more than 40 years of striper fishing experiences, I completely understand, as do so many others who pursue this fish, how striper fishing can cause people to ignore their jobs, their families, their sleep, and their warm and cozy surroundings in pursuit of the master of the surf. I'm sorry to say that my father died from cancer when I was 25, and before we could spend any significant time together fishing for stripers. Nevertheless, my striper experiences, and this book, are the result of his contagious enthusiasm for the challenge and mystique of surf fishing for this great fish and, an appropriate beginning for the pages that follow.

Through high school, and like most young teenage boys, my sights were set on cars, music, sports, beer and girls — and not necessarily in that order. Striper fishing had taken a back seat to the aforementioned pleasures until the day Bruce Shepley, one of my Princeton High School colleagues, mentioned that his parents were building a vacation house on some island in Rhode Island. I wasn't even sure where Rhode Island was, but it sure sounded promising. After all, a vacation house that was out of town..... where his parents *wouldn't* be on some weekends? That had "road trip with the girls" written all over it. But I actually forgot about it until one day when Bruce happened to mention to me that he had heard there was fantastic striper fishing around this island. The striper alarm that I had somehow managed to suppress for several years suddenly went off and I think it was the very next Friday that we left Princeton for a weekend on Jamestown (Conanicut) Island. I will never forget driving over the (old) Jamestown Bridge for the first time that Saturday morning at about 4 a.m. The bridge had one lane in each direction, but both lanes together seemed barely wide enough for one car, and the bridge was so high! No matter. With the advent of pristine shorelines and the promise of bass everywhere — Bruce and I were fired up. We decided that we'd drop our stuff off at the house and go right out to fish, despite the fact that we hadn't a clue as to where we were or where we were going. After waking up his parents, who were more or less (probably less) happy to see us at 4:30 in the morning, and after almost falling through the second-floor rafters, twice, in a house that was truly under construction, we left with frozen squid and surf rods in hand. Bruce decided that fishing from shore underneath the Jamestown Bridge might be the most practical thing to do, and so it was. I'll spare you the rest of the details, but suffice it to say that the only thing that we caught that night was cold and miserable. Little did we know, however, that Frank Daignault and his group were probably at the other end of the bridge, fishing *from the bridge*, and landing huge bass. But more on that later.

For those of you who are new to the sport, or have yet to try, take heart — we all have to start somewhere, and the beginning experiences of mine, and some of my very best friends (who compose what is now the Princeton Fishing Team), may amuse you. If you are a veteran surf caster, you too will relate to and muse at these beginnings, for no one becomes an expert overnight and certainly not without making mistakes. There's an old adage that says;

*"If every time you went fishing, the day was delightful, no problems were encountered and you caught as many fish as you wished, you would soon become bored with the sport and leave it for other pursuits."*

Lord knows that I've never come close to that consequence.

By my estimation, Jamestown and Block Island are to this day two of the finest places on earth — not only because of the splendid fishing opportunities that abound around the islands, but also because of their natural beauty, spectacular coastlines, and the fabulous history that envelops these two islands. When Bruce and I arrived on Jamestown Island (properly referred to as Conanicut Island) for the first time some 33 years ago, most of the roads were dirt roads that were heavily wash-boarded, and many of the paved roads weren't in great condition either. My Chevy Impala was never quite the same after that — the bone shaking Jamestown roads thoroughly altered the suspension. But who cared? We were after striped bass, and if that's what it took, fine. In those days, except for downtown Jamestown, the rest of the island was, for the most part, undeveloped. Beavertail, the southernmost end of the island and one of the best fishing spots for stripers, was heavily overgrown with thick brush and vines. There were only a handful of houses out on the "tail" and no paved parking areas next to the fishing spots as exist today. You had to either park at the Beavertail Lighthouse and navigate your way on foot over the rocky cliffs or, as most of the locals knew, you learned what paths along the side of the main road would lead you to some of the better fishing sections of Hull and Mackerel Coves.

Bruce and I weren't quite at that stage yet. After our first (and unsuccessful) attempt to catch fish from under the Jamestown Bridge, discovering that Bruce's father owned a boat was looking to be a pretty good alternative right about then. Bruce's parents, Bill and Mary Shepley, are of old-line Newport stock — both having grown up in Newport, attending the University of Rhode Island, and then moving to Princeton, New Jersey, to raise a family. I'm not sure how much Bill knew about fishing at that point, and judging from the condition of the boat and the fishing equipment in the basement...... well, let's just say that he was learning the sport along with the rest of us. I have to give him credit, though — at least he had his priorities in order. I was told that it wasn't uncommon for him to peer out into the West Passage of Narragansett Bay from the window of the Jamestown house, observe diving birds over the water, and then suddenly grab Mary and bolt for the boat, dropping any work on the house that he might have been doing. Bill knew that diving birds in the bay meant bass or bluefish, and that was a far greater priority than drywall installation — which, by the way, is one of the reasons the house took about 20 years to finish.

It was only a few weeks after my first weekend trip to Jamestown with Bruce that we both agreed to return for an entire week the next time. After all, it was the beginning of September and we would both be headed off to our first year of college soon. Having not caught anything on our first trip, but hearing from the locals that the striped bass fishing around the island was indeed excellent, we couldn't wait to return. This time, we decided to pay a visit to the local bait shop in order to get the skinny on where the fish were biting, and before adventuring off into untested waters.

That's when we met Rebelle.

Rebelle Felice owned and operated the island's only bait shop. The shop was basically a small, wooden shack on pilings and it was located on a tidal creek that runs east to west (depending upon the tide) from one side of the island to the other. The bait shop is still there today and it hasn't really changed much. Unfortunately, Rebelle passed away a few years back. He was one of the most opinionated, outspoken and charismatic people that I have ever met in my life (and that's putting it mildly). I never knew it was possible for anyone to spew so much profanity in a single sentence — sentence after sentence after sentence. I remember walking into the bait shop for the first time and having my attention immediately drawn to the photo board (also still there today) that was hung right next to the door. It was loaded with pictures of huge stripers, some by the truckload (there weren't any limits back then), and pictures of guys straining to hold up their huge fish for the camera. While I was looking at all these monster bass pictures, and being totally immersed in the notion that we had finally found striper paradise, I couldn't help overhearing the conversation that was taking place between Rebelle and another customer in the store. At first, I thought that they were having an argument because of the terse tone of the conversation, but then I realized — that was just Rebelle's style of communicating. Wow, what a mouth on this guy! I was only 17 at the time and I had never before heard anyone use so much foul language so often. Rebelle could have cussed the wallpaper right off the wall, but inside that crusty exterior was a soft guy with a big, big heart — although he sure fooled me the first day I met him and for some time after that. He didn't care much for "off-islanders," but since Bruce's parents were building a house on the island, well, that made us semi-acceptable. We asked him, with some trepidation, for advice on where we should go to try our luck the next morning to catch some stripers and I can't remember exactly where he directed us (most likely to hell). I do, however, remember him telling us that we needed to be wherever that was by 5 a.m.

Now, as a teenager, you didn't see 5 a.m. unless it was because you never went to bed the night before. So Bruce and I figured that Rebelle was just pulling our leg with the 5 o'clock thing and we decided that 8 a.m. or 9 a.m. would work just fine for us. As it turned out, Bruce's father had decided to let us take the boat out by ourselves the next morning. We were pretty excited about that, even though neither of us had ever driven a boat before, nor did we have any idea where we were going (isn't that a scary thought?). Although, we had some pretty nice equipment. It just so happened that by this time, *my* father had decided to convert to spinning gear and had commissioned one of his friends who was an expert rod builder to build a couple of custom surf rods for him. He had also purchased a few Penn 710 spinning reels to complete the outfits. However, if my father had ever discovered that I had brought *his* equipment to Rhode Island....... well, it would not have been pretty.

So off we went, into the West Passage of Narragansett Bay with two 10-foot *surf rods,* in a small boat, with plenty of frozen squid, and zero knowledge of the local waters. The Bay was suddenly looking very large. It didn't matter, though, because it was a calm sunny day and we remembered Bruce's father telling us that the Bay was deep, and that once we were a short distance offshore, it was unlikely that we would hit any submerged rocks. I can't remember what happened during the first few hours that morning, but I'm sure that we drowned a bunch of squid with little result. However, I will never forget what followed. Bruce was bored and frustrated that we weren't catching anything and so he decided to eat a sandwich. While he was sitting on top of the cooler eating his sandwich, he noticed something odd-looking in the water and at a considerable distance from the boat. He pointed it out to me and I agreed. There was a section of water, about as large as a small pond and about a quarter of a mile away from us that looked rippled and "nervous." We decided to go over and check it out. Sure enough, as we approached the area, it quickly became apparent that the ripples were being caused by fish. I don't know how we had the presence of mind to slow the boat down and approach this pod of fish at an idle, but we did. After all, as many an accomplished fisherman will tell you, it always seems that as soon as you manage to find a pod of feeding fish, some idiot in another boat will also see them and drive his boat right through the middle of the pod only to have the fish dive to the bottom and disappear. Fortunately, we were the only idiots out there on this day and at least we didn't make that mistake.

When we finally drifted close enough to this large circle of nervous water, we could see that the culprits causing all this commotion were indeed fish, but relatively small ones. They appeared to be about 15 to 20 inches long and between 2 and 4 pounds. Naturally, we immediately threw everything that we had in our tackle boxes at them (which wasn't much) — squid, jigs, metal — nothing worked. Geez, was this frustrating! Here were all these fish, literally hundreds of them, and they wouldn't so much as look at anything we presented. Finally, out of pure frustration, I suggested to Bruce that since the fish were so close together, I was going to put a treble (snag) hook on one of the lines in an effort to at least try to snag one so that we could find out what these fish were. Well, it worked like a charm, and what a surprisingly good fight these fish put up! Of course, the fact that I'd hooked most of them in the side *did* contribute to the battle. Upon seeing the ease of my success, Bruce immediately switched his rig to a treble hook and began to pull in these tough little fish as well. The action was fast and furious. Neither one of us had ever seen anything like it before — there we were, just hammering away at these fish, one after the other with *10-foot surf rods*, in a little boat, in the middle of the Bay. Nothing mattered; we were smiles from ear to ear. Fishing success, at last!

Now we still had no idea what we were catching, but we figured, hey, why not load up on them? We could get a cooler full of fish and then take them back to the bait shop to prove to Rebelle what accomplished fishermen we were. Yeah, right. Anyone who fishes the Bay knows that what we had encountered that day was a large school of menhaden. Menhaden can't be caught using traditional methods. The fish are vegetarians, they feed on phytoplankton and plant detritus, and they're rarely caught by rod and reel unless they're snagged. They are very important fish in the food chain, especially for stripers, but pretty much useless as table fare (in fact, I think the fillet board would taste better). But as any veteran of the surf knows, they make excellent bait, as we were just about to find out.

Our encounter with the menhaden went on for quite some time. We actually managed to fill the cooler to about three-quarter capacity when suddenly I noticed that I was having a bit more difficulty bringing in one of the snagged fish. In fact, this one started to run out line from the reel, and that's pretty tough on a Penn 710 with the drag even partially engaged. Bruce looked over and also noticed that the bend in my rod was far more significant — this fish was *really* fighting! Then the fish bolted out from under the menhaden school while remaining deep and out of sight. At least five minutes had passed (although it seemed like a half-hour to me) and I wasn't gaining anything on it. Bruce put down his rod and decided that we had better move the boat in the direction that the fish was going. Since the line that my father had spooled on this reel was only 12-pound test, that was probably a good idea. I don't remember how long I fought that fish, but it was indeed a battle. All the while, the fish stayed deep and we still didn't know what it was. Finally, I felt that I was gaining on it. Slowly, but still fighting, the fish started losing ground; it was almost at the boat now, but still deep. I will never forget seeing that fish surface from the deep, totally exhausted, and right alongside the boat. It was the biggest, meanest-looking fish that I had ever caught; however, it didn't have any stripes and I had no idea what it was. Bruce didn't know either. Neither one of us had ever seen a bluefish before, especially one this large. It looked as though it was pushing 20 pounds. The big blue was underneath all the menhaden and having a feast when it decided to go for one of the menhaden that I had snagged and it managed to inhale my treble hook at the same time.

Bruce and I had heard stories about how mean bluefish were supposed to be and how sharp their teeth were. Figuring that this was probably a bluefish, neither one of us was about to reach down and try to pull this alligator into the boat with our hands — a lot of guys have lost fingers trying to do that. And wouldn't you know it? We had no gaff or net on board! So Bruce grabbed the mooring pole and tried to get the curved end (which is used to retrieve mooring line) into the blue's mouth. Nothing doing. The fish wouldn't have any part of that. And although it was still exhausted, all this time we spent trying to figure out how to get it into the boat was giving the fish time to regain its strength, and the attempts to gaff it with the mooring pole had dislodged the hook's grasp so that just one prong of the treble hook was clinging, perilously, to the fish's upper lip. Knowing that we were running out of time, I decided to try to lift the fish in by the tail. Big mistake. About half of the way up, the big blue slipped out of my hand and back into the water. Out came the hook. The fish didn't discover right away that it was off, and it just stayed there, half-cocked to the side and looking up at us. Bruce and I quickly looked at each other with that stare of w*hat do we do now?* And then suddenly, the fish, realizing that it was no longer hooked, ever so slowly slunk away from the boat in a manner that clearly said "see ya later, boneheads." A beginner's first "catch and release" experience — well, sort of.

Of course, if we had known what we were doing, we would have kept each snagged menhaden in the water, hooked, and swimming for its life instead of loading an ice chest full of them. As any accomplished Bay fisherman will tell you, there were probably plenty of those hungry alligator blues underneath that school of menhaden and possibly some striped bass as well. It's a standard practice today, but back then….. well, as I said before — you have to start somewhere. Following that experience, and to this day, finding a menhaden school on the surface in the bay is cause for great excitement because, as we discovered a few years later, blues aren't the only fish found underneath these bait schools — sometimes it's the stripers that have come to the dinner table.

After venturing off to fight the bluefish, we never did find the menhaden school again that day, but we figured that we'd had enough action anyway, and besides, we had a cooler full of fish to take back and show off. When we arrived back at the house, Bruce's father wasn't around, but his mother, Mary, was very impressed with this great catch, although she wasn't sure what kind of fish these were either. So, off to the bait shop we went. We were proud of our fine catch and we were very much looking forward to finding out exactly what kind of fish they were. When we arrived at the bait shop, there were several other fishermen inside talking with Rebelle. As he was getting out some blood worms for one of the fishermen, we started to tell him about the large cooler full of fish that we had caught and that we didn't know what they were. Rebelle was only half-paying attention to us, but he blurted out; "Go head, bring 'em in here — let's see what yez got." Excited to have the opportunity to boast, we brought the cooler into the shop and, of course, all eyes were then upon us. Meanwhile, Bruce and I, in all of our excitement, didn't even think to put the fish on ice. They were in the cooler alright, but accumulating fishy stench by the minute. Well, it didn't take but a second after we had opened the cooler for a loud roar of laughter to emanate from all present in the shop (except, of course, from us). "What are you guys laughing at?" I asked. "Je…sus… Christ!" barked Rebelle. "Get that God damn stinkin f___ bait outta here….#@!?*#!" Needless to say, after that, we totally understood the menhaden's purpose in the fishing world — which was not as a trophy picture on the bait shop photo board.

Just before we left the shop, we asked Rebelle if he had gone fishing that morning. I remember him looking back at us with a face that plainly said *you silly boys* as he walked over to a large tub and pulled back a piece of burlap just far enough to expose a bunch of very large bass tails — *on ice*. He then looked up at us with a half-smile and said, "Hey, where were you guys at 5 this morning anyway?"

# Chapter II

## Raymond

It was during the next summer following my introduction to Jamestown that Raymond Pettus arrived on the fishing scene. Raymond lived around the block from me in Princeton and at the time, we were both attending Princeton High School. From high school to this day, Raymond has been one of my very best friends and one of Bruce's very best friends as well. At school, he was one grade behind Bruce and me, but when it came to fishing luck, for almost 20 years he was absolutely behind everyone. Raymond was named "Best Personality" in the high school yearbook and, after spending just a little time with him, it's easy for anyone to understand why he deserved this title (and the fish would certainly have agreed — for many years he was exceptionally kind to them as well). Raymond has always been Mr. Congeniality: liked by everyone, kind-hearted, jovial, and full of cheap one-liners — some of which we've heard over and over and over again, but somehow, he just has a way of making them laughable every time.

Bruce and I had relayed our first Jamestown fishing experiences to Raymond and encouraged him to join us on our next trip. He was all ears and very excited about the opportunity. Until then, I hadn't realized how much he was actually interested in fishing. Bruce and I had also told our fishing stories to quite a few of our other friends, especially the girls. We figured what could be better than a fishing paradise, beer, and girls all in the same place? As a result, there were many trips from Princeton to Jamestown, sometimes with several carloads of teenagers, packed with fishing equipment, spearfishing equipment, and plenty of beer. Being the enterprising teens that we were (isn't it amazing how teenagers can be that way when they really want to?), we were quick to figure out that although the drinking age in New Jersey and Rhode Island was 21, in New York it was 18. So as it turned out, it was mighty convenient that we had to pass through New York on the way to Rhode Island. Bruce's parents, Bill and Mary, probably had second thoughts about opening the doors of their Jamestown vacation house to Bruce and company, especially after the time we arrived in four cars with 15 kids. But nevertheless, they always welcomed us with open arms and they seemed to enjoy all the extra chaos and excitement.

Since teenagers usually don't have the slightest interest in seeing the hour of 5 a.m., there wasn't a whole lot of successful striper fishing done in those early years by our gang — especially by Raymond, but I'll get to that later. And night fishing often took a back seat to beer drinking and carrying on, which had the predictable result of making the 5 a.m. sunrise even less of a possibility for fishing. I remember one afternoon when Bruce, Raymond, and I managed to sneak into the Narragansett Café, even though we weren't old enough to drink. On the other hand, back then, I doubt that anyone in bar really cared. Although I'm sure that's not the case today. The other friends who had joined us on this trip had decided to take a break and were back at the house. The Narragansett Café is located in downtown Jamestown on Narragansett Avenue. In those days, it was very much a local watering hole and was usually packed with crusty old fishermen and sailors. Mothers warned their children to walk on the other side of the street because the door was usually propped open and you never knew what sort of comments might come flying out, not to mention an inebriated patron now and then (although the patrons usually got knocked through the large multi-paned window in the front, which is why it was so often covered with a piece of plywood). Somehow we managed to be served a few beers that afternoon and, while we were sitting at one of the tables drinking to our success, one of the other patrons in the bar overheard our conversation and offered his advice. I had been speaking with Raymond and wondering how we might be able to catch some lobsters. I guess this old fisherman and his buddies saw that they had a few gullible kids at their mercy and decided to have some fun. The guy leaned over to us and said that he had managed to catch a nice bunch of lobsters just the night before, and if we'd be kind enough to buy a round of beer for him and his pals, he'd tell us where to look. No problem. A few beers in return for some lobster secrets? Are you kidding? We were all ears. He told us that you could only get the lobsters at night and at low tide. He instructed us to go out to Hull Cove at the bottom of the tide and to bring flashlights. He explained that the lobsters would crawl out of the sea and onto the rocks, where we could blind them with the flashlights and then pick them up and put them in our buckets. Wow, lobster dinner, here we come. We raced back to the house to report the news to the others and to see how many flashlights we could find. Not long after dark, 15 kids were pushing their way through the mosquito-laden brush on the road out to Hull Cove, flashlights and buckets in hand. Of course, by the time we discovered we'd been had, it was many mosquito bites and an hour of searching the rocks later. On the other hand, several of us had noticed that although there were no lobsters, there *were* lots of green crabs, so we decided to take them home instead. After all, crabmeat was good too, right? When we arrived back at the house, Bruce's father, Bill, was in the basement working on something as we all piled out of the cars and made our way through the garage door, into the basement, and up the steps to the first floor. On my way upstairs, Bill asked me how many lobsters we had managed to catch. When I told him none, he asked what was in the bucket. I showed him the green crabs and he almost passed out. Almost every one was an undersized female with eggs — about 40 in all. So Bill summoned Bruce down into the basement (Bruce was the one who always got into trouble for what everyone else did), and we were ordered to take the crabs back down to the bay and release them immediately. I think Bill said that if we had been caught with those crabs, the fine for taking females was $25 per crab — enough to buy how many lobsters and how much beer? Needless to say, that was the last advice we ever took from anyone in the Narragansett Café, fishing or otherwise.

One of the advantages, in addition to much better striper fishing, that the waters around Jamestown had over those of the Jersey shore was clarity. The bay water in the New Jersey tidal areas always seemed to have low visibility, whereas the coastal waters surrounding Jamestown were almost always clear. Much to our disappointment, we discovered that stripers don't very often feed during the day, so our daytime summer activities were focused more on skin-diving and spearfishing for other types of fish. The guys would snorkel and spearfish while the girls would sunbathe on the rocks. I was always amazed by how much active marine life we found just a few feet from shore. We never had to swim out more than 15 or 20 yards and rarely were we in water more than 10 feet deep. It's no wonder that bass and bluefish forage the shorelines; the inshore waters are teeming with small fish and other organisms. Bruce and I discovered that one of the fish that we frequently encountered, the blackfish (known locally as a tautog), was particularly slow to avoid our spears. Blackfish are curious by nature, which often made them easy targets for the grill — and tasty fare they are, too. It's interesting that considering all the summer days that we spent diving around Jamestown, we never saw a shark and we rarely got a glimpse of a passing striper. Of course, one of the contributing factors to the scarcity of striper sightings was probably the fact that those were the early years of the big decline in the overall bass population. Small bass tend to hang close to shore, even during the day. The big fish came in at night. Unfortunately, we weren't even seeing many small fish while diving during those years, and that turned out to be a harbinger of things to come.

Today if you dive these waters you're very likely to see a good number of small to medium-sized stripers, and a lot of guys do very well spearfishing for them. If you've never tried skin-diving in the waters off Jamestown and Block Island, you don't know what a great experience you're missing. The only caution I would offer is to make sure to pick a day with mild surf. When we became more experienced, we switched from diving in secluded coves to diving from the rocks off the east side of Beavertail. We found a lot more fish there and they were bigger as well. But sometimes the surf is just too rough out there and it doesn't take much to get body-slammed by a big wave into the barnacle-encrusted rocks. When that happens, if you're lucky enough not to be knocked out, the barnacles will make you pay the price just the same. You just have to use good judgment regarding when to go, and when not to go into the water out at the "tail."

Somewhere in my photo albums, I have a picture of Raymond standing on top of a half-submerged rock about 15 yards offshore, holding a 4-foot-long wooden garden stake with a four-pronged frog gig haphazardly attached to one end. Impaled by the prongs of the gig was a "chaggie," a trash fish, which was a whopping 5 inches long and which had taken him the better part of the afternoon to spear. The picture is perfectly emblematic of Raymond's early luck as a fisherman, but unfortunately for him, that kind of luck lasted for about 20 years after that. I don't know anyone who has ever had such a long string of horrible luck when it comes to fishing. On more occasions than not, when the fishing was slow or nonexistent for all of us, immediately following Raymond's departure from the island, everyone who remained would start catching fish. It just happened all the time.

I can't think of a better example of this than the day Bruce and I took Raymond to the train station in West Kingston (on the RI mainland) one late September afternoon. The three of us had been fishing the shores of Jamestown for two or three days and Raymond had to return early to Princeton. Bruce and I decided to stay and fish for one more day, although the fishing up until that point had been very slow. Bruce and I had managed to catch a few small bluefish, but that was about it. So we put Raymond on a train headed back to Princeton and decided to get an early dinner at the Ratskeller, a restaurant which was located near the train station. Since there were still three hours of daylight remaining, we figured that we could get dinner out of the way and then fish the sunset on into the night. As it turns out, the Ratskeller was routinely closed one day each week, and this was it. Little did we know that Raymond's departure was already beginning to shine its good fortune upon us. We said the hell with dinner, and decided to go fishing instead. Our destination was the fishing area in front of the Point Judith Lighthouse. When we arrived at the point, we were surprised to find that the surf was full of whitewater and was actually starting to kick up quite a bit. The wind was coming in from the south at about 15 knots and a cloud cover had moved in. It really felt like some significant weather was coming. We were also delighted to discover that no one was out there but us that evening and so we positioned ourselves on the left and right side drop-offs of the south cove.

What happened next would later be recorded as some of the most exciting fishing that Bruce and I had ever experienced. With Raymond well along on his journey back to Princeton, fishing success for me and Bruce was almost a certainty. I was using the standard-issue blue-and-white Atom popper, and I'm not sure what Bruce had on. I really don't think it would've mattered. After you've fished the surf for a few years, you start to understand what the term "good-looking water" means; and the water that afternoon had fish written all over it. The conditions were as good as it gets. There was a good wind (but not too much of it), lots of whitewater, cloud cover, and approaching dusk. We could both sense that something was going to happen. And sure enough it did. We hadn't taken more than three casts when wham! I got a huge hit right at the end of my cast and I was onto a fish. The fish started running line off the reel and I could really feel that it had some weight to it. I turned to Bruce with my rod almost bent in half and whistled over to him, and just as he looked over in my direction, he had a strike and was then connected to a fish as well. After a reasonably tough fight, I maneuvered my fish in close enough to see that it was a huge bluefish. The fish had turned sideways in the breaker line (as they somehow always know how to do) and was using the back-pull of the back side of the waves to fight against me. This is the point where over-anxious surf fishermen, both inexperienced and experienced, sometimes lose their fish because the heavy backwash of water receding from a breaker can easily exert enough additional force to pull the fish free. It's a game of constantly adjusting your drag, using the incoming waves to pull your fish onto the beach at just the right moment, and above all, having patience. I felt that this blue was starting to tire, so with the next approaching breaker, I pulled it into the crest of the wave and then used the wave and the rod to pull the fish up onto the beach as the wave crashed in. It was a big, beautiful bluefish that appeared to weigh in the upper teens. I dragged it up high onto the beach and then went back down to the surf to cast for more. It was just starting to get dark at this point, but I looked over and I could still see Bruce fighting his fish. I gave him a thumbs up and tried to yell over to him that my fish was a bluefish, but the roar of the surf was too loud for him to hear me, so I started casting once again. On the very next cast I was immediately onto another fish. As I peered down the beach, I could see Bruce dragging his fish up onto the rocks and looking over to see my rod bent once again. We both knew we were into the fish big-time!

This was my first experience with what is, of course, commonly referred to as a blitz. Neither Bruce nor I had ever seen anything quite like it before. The blues were hitting on nearly every cast and both of us were beginning to accumulate nice piles of fish behind us. These fish were all in the high ‘teens’ weight class and they were fighting like pit bulls on steroids — probably because, as we would find out later, they had trapped a school of menhaden in the little cove where we were fishing and as a delectable consequence, they had been feeding on pure protein for a few hours.

Bluefish are voracious feeders. They'll gorge themselves until the bait pours out of their gills and then still won't be able to resist hitting a plug. True to form, in just a few hours’ time, we had scored a huge bunch of very nice bluefish in an action-packed, all-out blitz, but the bluefish had also managed to take their revenge on our equipment. I had lost more than a few lures and, although I didn’t know it, Bruce had just lost the last plug that he had. So with that, Bruce decided to walk down the beach and see if I had any spare lures in my surf bag. He was walking in my direction and, although I couldn't see him, out of the dark night I heard him yelling, "Raymond! Raymond! Thank you! Raymond!" For it had become commonplace that when Raymond left, the fish arrived — and that night was certainly no exception.

Today, I rarely, if ever, keep bluefish. They're oily and way too strong for my taste. I'm also so much more cognizant in my older years of the necessity to conserve the resource — in contrast to how I thought about it when I was younger. Sometimes at an early age you just don't understand the importance of conservation or the consequences of indifference. And so it was that night. When Bruce and I finally decided to stop fishing, we realized that we had each caught about a dozen bluefish, all weighing over 15 pounds. It turned out that it was actually about 400 pounds of fish that we had to get back to the car, which was located more than 300 yards away. The excitement of catching the fish was just too great; we'd never once given a thought to dealing with all these fish afterwards.

When we arrived back at the house at 2:30 that morning, we had so many fish, and we were so tired, that we had to use a wheelbarrow to get the blues out of the car (which was really starting to smell ripe by then) and into the basement. This was the largest single catch that had ever been scored by anyone at the house and it was a cause for great celebration. I remember that Bruce's father came down into the basement in his bathrobe to see what was going on. He became so excited when he saw all the fish, that he took over and filleted every single one of them. I can only imagine what that bathrobe must have smelled like when he returned to his bedroom; I think it walked by itself to the washing machine the next morning.

Poor Raymond. You just know that he was the first person we called the next day. But as I mentioned before, this always seemed to be the kind of luck that followed Raymond — or at least his departure.

**The author and Bruce Shepley with some of the bluefish caught during the night of the great Point Judith blitz.**

One Saturday afternoon a few years before the Point Judith blitz, Bruce, Raymond, and I were fishing from the rocks off of Hazard Avenue, just south of Jamestown and on the mainland. There were several schools of "harbor blues" (the fishermen's nickname for small bluefish) that were working underneath some bait pods just beyond the rocks, and every now and then the bluefish would come within casting distance. We were standing on a rather long flat rock, with me positioned at one end, Raymond in the middle, and Bruce on the other end, and we were all using metal Kastmasters for lures. Over a period of about and hour and a half, Bruce and I were pretty much alternating hookups each time the fish came in. And Raymond..... well, you guessed it — not so much as a bump. Even though he was fishing right between Bruce and me! Then, as it appeared that the fish had moved offshore once again, we all decided to sit down for a beer break. We left the rods lying on the rock exactly in the positions where each one of us had been standing in order to save our spots because there were a lot of other guys out there fishing that morning. As we were enjoying our beer, Bruce started to tease Raymond about not catching anything while cynically pointing out to him that it had to be the consequence of a deficiency in a certain fisherman's level of skill and ability, especially since all the equipment was identical. Raymond countered that he was at a disadvantage by having to stand in the middle. Hearing that, Bruce stood up, walked over to Raymond's rod, which was still lying in the middle position, and said, "Watch this." Sure enough, as soon as the lure hit the water, Bruce was onto a fish. Bruce and I were laughing so hard that we had trouble standing up. If only you could have seen the look of disbelief on Raymond's face — it was priceless!

Raymond was also the king of equipment failure. It was a sure bet that any piece of fishing equipment he touched was doomed to break, leak, crack, snap off, or seize up. I don't think that, until recently, he has ever had a pair of waders that didn't leak and that weren't two sizes too small for him. Sometimes it took Bruce and me working together to pull Raymond's waders off of him and, of course, the suction of the water inside didn't make things any easier. His fishing rod was a Raymond original. The spongy grip material on the rod butt had deteriorated to the point where the stuff was cracking and beginning to fall off. To prevent this from happening further, Raymond had duct-taped the entire rod butt all the way up to the reel. It was a sight to behold. His reel was an old Diawa that appeared to weigh about 2 pounds and sounded as if there were marbles inside when it was cranked.

I remember one night when Raymond and I were fishing at the mouth of the Narrow River in Narragansett. We were standing in our rubber chest waders, fairly far out into the mouth of the river and in about waist-deep water, fishing with Danny swimmer plugs. Raymond had managed to hook his first striped bass ever. Although it wasn't a very big fish, it still would have been an amazing turn of events if he had landed it. But of course as his luck would have it, the fish started circling around Raymond as he reeled it closer, all the while trying to be extra careful not to put much pressure on it for fear of pulling the hooks. Seeing this, another fisherman who was standing close to Raymond came over to help with a hand gaff. That fish must have circled Raymond at least five times with the other fisherman in pursuit, slapping away at the water with the gaff, trying to impale the fish — it was comical at best. Finally, the gaff hit Raymond's line, the line broke, and the fish took off.

At the end of the night, as Raymond and I were walking down Narragansett Town Beach on the way back to our car, I kept hearing an unusual sound. I wasn't sure where it was coming from so I asked him if he could hear it also. He said; "Sure..... it's about two gallons of the ocean in the left boot of my waders and another gallon in the right one." Another classic Raymond evening.

Probably the most hilarious fishing experience I've ever had in my life was the day Raymond hooked a building. With his incredible predisposition for bad luck and mishaps now well entrenched, Raymond, Bruce, and Bill and I were out in Bill's boat one morning, fishing some of Narragansett Bay's "hot spots" in the East Passage between Jamestown and Newport. This was many years and two or three boats after Bill's first boat, and *this* boat was custom-designed for fishing the bay with lots of room for casting. Bill was being the guide and good captain that he always was while Raymond, Bruce and I were casting artificials to the spot of the moment. Our technique was a good one and it works quite well to this day. Bill would slowly guide the boat down a section of rocky shoreline, just within casting distance from shore, moving in and out at idle speed. The others on board would be casting into the whitewater caused by the breaking of the waves against the rocks. We covered a lot of territory this way and we managed to hit some pretty nice fish now and then. I have also seen lots of guys using this technique out on Block Island, slinging eels and artificials into the rocky nooks and crannies of the surf. On the Block, however, you really need to know what you're doing — especially along the south shore. That shoreline is loaded with submerged rocks, and the waves are merciless if you get too close.

In Jamestown, one of our favorite spots to fish in the East Passage was along the north point of Gould Island. The island was used by the government during World War II for manufacturing and testing torpedoes. The Navy would actually test-fire torpedoes out into the bay from torpedo tubes that were attached to the building (God only knows how many torpedoes are still sitting on the bottom out there — no wonder it's a "no anchor" zone). In order to accomplish this, the Navy had to extend part of the building over the water on concrete pilings and, as one might guess, those pilings often hold lots of baitfish, which attract bluefish and stripers. We arrived at Gould about midmorning on that day and we were all casting to the pilings on the west side of the island. Bruce and I hooked a couple of small blues almost as soon as we got there, so the level of anticipation was climbing. As we rounded the northernmost point of the island, the 20-foot metal stanchions supporting the torpedo tubes came into view (it's quite an eerie and imposing sight when you see it for the first time). We started to cast in and around the stanchions that had held fish in the past when, suddenly, a very loud metal clang rang out across the water. I turned around to look into the boat, and there was Raymond, standing, rod bent, and with a disgusted "not me again" look on his face. By this time, Bruce was laughing uncontrollably. I turned back to see what had happened and there, about 15 feet up on one of the torpedo stanchions, was Raymond's metal Kastmaster, solidly attached. Yes, Raymond had managed to hook the building. In typical Raymond fashion, his lure had wrapped itself around a thin pipe that was attached to one of the torpedo stanchions, and then to make things worse, it back-hooked his line with its own hook — it would have been impossible for anyone else, but not for Raymond. After many laughs and the use of the mooring pole to finally free his lure, the day Raymond caught a building will never be forgotten (we've all made sure of that).

To Raymond's credit, he has since become an accomplished and experienced surf fisherman with top-notch equipment, including sharpened hooks, waders that don't leak and a meticulously organized surf bag. He has a driving passion for the sport as well as a deep appreciation for the natural beauty of Block Island and Jamestown, and I must say that I have been fortunate to have shared some of life's finest fishing experiences with him on both islands, including one of the biggest striper blitzes I've ever seen. But more on that later.

# Chapter III

## The Block

It was during the mid- to late '70s when I started fishing on Block Island. I remember that the bass population had begun a noticeable decline at the time and it was becoming increasingly more difficult to consistently find striped bass along the shores of mainland Rhode Island. In spite of the declining striper numbers, reports were consistently coming in from Block Island that were quite to the contrary. The bass fishing out on the Island was said to be exceptional, especially the fall run, and most of the fish were reported to be very large. Likewise, getting bluefish out on the Block was supposed to be almost a sure bet, and word had it that the blues out on the Block were also running on the large side.

I was attending graduate school at the University of Rhode Island at the time and several of my student colleagues were also avid fishermen. In fact, I was surprised by how many URI grad students were into striper fishing. It was almost a certainty that class size would be noticeably diminished on any given day during the fall when rainy or cloudy weather moved in (bass activity always increased with the onset of inclement weather). I remember one of the pharmacology professors looking around the room over the top of his glasses at the beginning of a lecture one rainy day. Upon noticing the reduced attendance, he remarked, "Hmmm.... guess the bass are in."

One of my student colleagues at URI enjoyed fishing for bluefish and he began making trips out to the Block once or twice a week during the fall. He would come to class with reports of bonanza bluefish catches so often that he finally convinced me to go out to the island and see for myself.

On my first trip there, I made the mistake of going to the island on a sunny day, at low tide, and too early in the fall season. Lacking any knowledge of where to fish, I fished Crescent Beach that afternoon (it was a short walk from the ferry). It's not that Crescent Beach is a bad spot, but there are much more historically productive places to fish. Although at low tide and on a sunny day, I'm not so sure that a beach chair and a beer wouldn't have been a better idea altogether. In reality, if I had been an accomplished striper fisherman at the time, I wouldn't have visited the island during the day and would instead have arrived at sunset to fish through the night. But at the time, daylight was more appealing and the beach just seemed like the easiest place to go. Fortunately, my lack of success on that afternoon didn't deter me from heading out to the island once again.

As it turns out, I was not the first off-islander to hear the reports that the bass fishing on the Block was first-rate. There were lots of guys coming over to the island in the fall from New York and Connecticut as well as from mainland Rhode Island. The Block Islanders had known for more than two centuries what fertile fishing grounds surrounded their precious island and they weren't especially happy about off-islanders coming over and taking *their* fish. Not unless, of course, you were a patron of one of the hotels or bed and breakfasts — then you were quasi-acceptable.

I discovered later that some of the Block Islanders had a particular dislike for a few of the fishermen from New York. Apparently several of the New York guys were leaving trash around the island and had an attitude of general disrespect for the locals. On the other hand, most of the New York fishermen were knowledgeable surfcasters and were quite conscious of the fragility of the fishing resources and the environment. Nonetheless, it seems that there were a few bad apples and so one day, in an attempt to bring one of the culprits to an "understanding," some of the Block Island boys set up a "tank trap" for one of the New York fishermen who needed an attitude adjustment. Some of the local guys got together and used a backhoe to dig out a trench on the road leading to Southwest Point where, as it just so happened, this guy from New York always fished. It was right after a very rainy period and so the road was already full of very large water-filled potholes. When they filled the trench they had dug with water, it simply looked like another large puddle. However, *this* puddle was about 5 feet deep. The local guys spread the word to all the other fishermen about the trap and then waited for the New York guy to head out to the Point. When his front wheels hit the hole, half of his truck went down into the water-filled crater and he was stuck there for the night. Rumor had it that his truck was in the "tank trap" for a reasonably long stay because he couldn't find anyone on the island to pull him out...... imagine that?

Prior to my journeys to the Block, I never had the experience of putting my car on a boat. The process is a little unnerving until you get used to it because you have to back your car onto the boat — with little room for error. On my first trip, they loaded on more cars on the boat than I thought the boat could safely handle, followed by two giant tractor-trailers that backed their way onto the last remaining space on the car deck. Seeing this, I remember thinking, "There's no way this boat's going to handle all this weight, it's going down with the first big wave — what have I gotten myself into?" Of course, it was an uneventful trip and the ferry made it to the island, as usual and right on time. Since that trip, I have taken at least several hundred more and my level of confidence in the boats and their crew couldn't be higher. I have even enjoyed some challenging seas now and then, which tends to make the excursion more exciting — but that's because I have never fallen prey to seasickness (I'm sure those in the green-faced line in front of the boat's restrooms will curse me).

In fact, that reminds me of a most incredible ride over to the island one late October afternoon. I've never seen anything like it since and I guess that's a good thing, but it sure was interesting and amusing at the time. I was on one of the smaller boats. It was a Friday afternoon and the ferry was loaded with tourists going over to the island in hopes of enjoying a nice fall weekend. I'm not sure why there were so many people on the boat because the forecast was predicting a wet weekend with heavy surf and wind from the south. At the time the boat left, the winds were already approaching 30 knots and the swells were large and building. As the ferry emerged from between the Point Judith break-walls, it became apparent that we were headed into seas of 8 to 10 feet — a prospect not in the least appealing when you're on one of the smaller ferries. The boat was so packed with weekenders that several dozen of them had positioned themselves, along with their bags and suitcases, along the outside walkways of the main cabin, all the way around the bow, and down the starboard and port sides. The weather was windy, but mild, and I guess these folks were thinking that it would be better to take in some fresh air rather than remain in the crowded cabin. I was standing half in and half out of the starboard door on the first deck, peering out at the amazing swells that we were headed into. We hadn't gone more than a half-mile beyond the breakwater when suddenly the captain eased back on the throttle of the diesel engines to prepare the boat for what was ahead. Sensing that something was about to happen, I stuck my head out of the doorway just in time to see the first of three rogue 15-footers headed straight at the bow. I ducked back inside and turned to the guy standing next to me and said "Watch this!" No sooner had the words left my mouth than did the bow of the ship spear its nose into the first of the three huge swells, sending a wall of the Atlantic over the front of the ship and down each side of the boat, thoroughly soaking every tourist out there — and then twice more before any of them had the chance to react. As the water cleared from the porthole windows, all that could be seen through the water-laced glass were completely soaked weekenders with straightened wet hair, saturated luggage, and astonished looks on their faces. Needless to say, there were long lines in front of the restrooms for the rest of that trip, and not surprisingly, it was the last boat that ran for the next two days.

On my second journey out to the Block, I decided to do it right. I took my station wagon (do they even make those anymore?) over to the island and I was going to fish for a few days this time. I had asked one of my URI colleagues to join me, but he had other plans. Upon learning that I was heading over to the Block, he made a comment that stirred my curiosity. He said that I ought to do well on the fishing side of things, but that the people out there were kind of strange. I thought that I should know more about that, so I asked him to explain. He began his explanation with the story of the Palatine shipwreck and ended with the comment that the locals really don't like off-islanders coming over and catching "their" fish. For those of you who aren't familiar with the story of the Palatine, suffice it to say that the legend tends to paint a pretty mean picture of some of the early Block Islanders. The precise account of exactly what happened to the ship remains in dispute and the mystery lives on. As the story goes, sometime between 1700 and 1750, a small group of pirates would come ashore at night and position lanterns atop strategic positions on one of the island bluffs. To vessels sailing in the distance, the false beacons looked like another ship and this would entice such passing ships to follow in hopes of safe passage. Instead, they would sail right into the dangerous rocks that surrounded the island and, once aground, the rough surf would finish the job. The ship's bounty would then wash ashore to the benefit of these pirates (who were actually not Block Islanders at all). And so it was with the Palatine; however, in this instance, it was alleged that there were many of the ship's survivors to deal with and, well..... I'll leave the rest to your imagination. My friend's stories were all that I needed to hear to give a mysterious slant to the island. It was quite apparent that I wouldn't be greeted out there with a Hawaiian lei and tropical cocktails.

I never really considered the boat trip to be a deterrent. There were suppose to be big bass out there and I was determined to find them. And the second time I decided to make the trip I had a light schedule at URI for the next few days so I took a boat over during the middle of the week. It was mid-October and it was cool and very foggy. Fog always has the effect of giving things an eerie appearance, not to mention the spooky effect it has by muting noise with its atmospheric thickness. Well, this was *just* what I needed. In light of all the stories I'd heard about the island, the visual effect created by the fog was holding the image true to my imagination. It was soooo quiet and mysterious-looking as the ferry slowly glided into Old Harbor. It was late in the season, the tourists were all gone, and in the fog, the now-vacant National Hotel looked like a giant haunted house looming above the town. The ferry docked, and the cars drove onto the island one by one. As I drove off the ferry and onto the dock, I happened to glance over to the left and then had to do an immediate double take. I couldn't believe my eyes. I pulled over and stopped the station wagon to get out and look more closely. There, next to the shipping and receiving area of the Interstate Navigation office, were several burlap-covered pallets stacked almost 5 feet high. What had caught my attention was the fact that, sticking out from under the burlap, were dozens of large fishtails. Then I realized that the pallets were loaded with huge stripers that had been caught the night before, tagged, and destined for off-island processing and sale. This was the first time I had ever seen this many striped bass. And these fish were cows, none appearing to be less than 30 pounds. My curiosity did not go unnoticed as I quickly got a few "what are you looking at?" stares from the local dock workers. I took the hint and got back into the station wagon, but I was thrilled to confirm that indeed the island had big stripers in its waters and plenty of them. From that day forward, the majority of my striper fishing has been done on the Block.

Learning the island wasn't easy. After all, anyone who's familiar with the Block, even today, knows that there's essentially one road that encircles the island, which in very few places allows direct access to the water. And after hearing all the stories surrounding the "locals," I was very apprehensive about walking or driving through someone's property considering what the consequences might be relative to the island's history (at least what I had erroneously contrived).

As a last resort, I decided to pay a visit to the only bait shop on the island. The shop was owned and managed by the late Mac Swienton. Mac's experience, personality, and contributions to life on Block Island are so significant that I've devoted a good deal of well-deserved space to him later in this book. Suffice it to say that he was a pleasure to speak with and he took a sincere interest in trying to direct me to some very good island fishing spots. Trouble was, I only half-believed him, thinking that he, like most locals, would want to deceive me so I wouldn't return. Not so. Mac was genuine and honest, and he actually tried to direct me to the spots where he had heard fish were caught the night before. One of the locations that he suggested I try was Southwest Point. I had no idea where that was, but since I didn't want to look like a rookie in front of Mac, I gave him a polite "thanks for the tip" nod and said that I'd give it a try later that night. Well, I never managed to find Southwest Point, so I fished the beach in front of Ballard's (next to the Old Harbor ferry landing) that evening and didn't catch a thing.

The next morning the fog had lifted and it turned into a rather nice autumn day. I again set out to find Southwest Point. If you're new to fishing on Block Island, or just plain new to fishing for that matter, one thing that you'll discover is that it's pretty much a "fishermen's universal code" that, other than to your very best friends, you never give up the exact location of a great fishing spot. There are several reasons for this. First, for your own benefit, if you don't want to see a dozen other guys standing in *your* spot the next time you go there, you'd best be somewhat ambiguous regarding exactness and, second, there's just something amazingly self-satisfying about finding a successful spot on your own. Well, that's kind of how it was discovering the Block. For instance, the first time I was directed to Black Rock, I expected to see a giant black rock and, supposedly, that was where you fished. Not so. The Black Rock area is huge and there are multiple locations that are good fishing spots along the entire length of the shoreline.

I was still having no success in finding Southwest Point. I was expecting at least a sign (to one of the island's best fishing spots? Oh sure, fat chance). I finally broke down and asked for directions from a couple of islanders who were working on a utility pole on the side of Coonymus Road. They both looked at me as though I were from another planet (as if to say, "You don't know where Southwest Point is?"), but nonetheless, they cordially gave me specific directions, and sure enough, I ended up exactly where I needed to be. So much for the less-than-congenial reputation that I thought the islanders had. Today, the Point is surrounded by many new houses and you can't drive there as in the past. Access is by way of Coonymus Road and then by walking the shoreline. But back in the '70s, there were very few houses out there. It was mostly vacant fields and a single dirt road that meandered precariously close to the bluff edge leading directly to the point. When I arrived at the Point for the first time, there, off the road and in the brush, was an abandoned Chevy of late '50s vintage. Someone had taken a broken-off keel from a surfboard and attached it like a dorsal fin to the roof of the car, giving it an ominous and evil land-shark appearance. I remember thinking to myself, "Oh man, they're really wild out here — what have I gotten myself into?" Nevertheless, I headed down the path to the water because Mac Swienton had told me to make sure to arrive early, before the line started. I wasn't sure what he was talking about, although it didn't take long to find out. It was about 4 in the afternoon when I arrived. Of course, in mid-October, that wasn't too long before sunset. At that moment, I was the only one there, so I didn't give Mac's comment any further thought.

For many years, and until I discovered what really worked on stripers, I almost always used top water popper plugs. The blue-and-white Atom Popper was my plug of choice. I had fished with eels and chunks of menhaden before, but the sporting challenge of fishing with artificials has always been a lot more fun. That's not to say that eels aren't effective because, as any accomplished surfcaster will tell you, they're deadly. However, there is nothing more exciting than seeing a fish smash a lure on the surface of the water (during the day, of course). I had used the Atom Popper so often that I became exceptionally adept at retrieving it at just the right speed, and with just the right action, so that it was very enticing to just about anything that crossed its path. So often you see guys working a popper so fast across the surface of the water that even the high-speed ferry couldn't catch it. The correct retrieve is actually a slow jerk-and-stop, jerk-and-stop motion that produces a good-sized forward splash with every pull — and to bluefish, that's simply irresistible. Unfortunately, the bass weren't nearly as enthralled with poppers as the bluefish were and as a consequence, I caught so many bluefish for so many years — and very few bass — that I started to realize that I needed to change something. I finally caught on after my first night at Southwest Point taught me one of the most important bass lessons I ever learned.

So, there I was at the famous Southwest Point, casting with my popper, and with no one else around. I was still wondering what all the fuss was about over getting there early. I had been casting for about 45 minutes and I had the place all to myself. As I was basking in my solitude, and watching the sunset, the first of several trucks arrived at what I later learned is called "Fishermen's Landing," and transporting large troops of fishermen. The surf conditions that night were as good as it gets for your first time out at the Point — light wind, fairly warm, and a moderate wave pattern. For anyone who has never fished the Point — take heart — it ain't for the inexperienced on anything other than a very calm night. The wave action at the Point, coupled with a minefield of small submerged rocks that are like walking on bowling balls with dishwashing liquid poured over them, presents a challenging environment for any angler. And, except during high tide, you really need to stand in the water to cast to the best spots. The waves at the Point come at you from three directions and, just when you think that you've got your feet planted for a good casting stance, you're likely to lose your balance and have to reposition. It's a constant battle with the waves, the rocks, and the wind. Investing in a pair of Korkers, or the lightweight Stream Cleats from L.L. Bean, gives you a real advantage with this type of bottom. The spikes on these slip-ons will cut right through the slimy surface of the rocks and they really help you to establish more stable footing. The waves on the other hand….. well, good luck!

Now, the fishing protocol and etiquette that I was used to apparently didn't apply at the Point. For instance, unless you're good friends with the guy next to you or unless there's a substantial blitz in progress, it is generally understood that you give another fisherman at least 30 or 40 yards' distance. If he was there first, the spot is his until he leaves, and that includes not jumping into his spot just because he has to drag a fish ashore. It's a different story at Southwest Point. It's not uncommon to see fishermen standing shoulder to shoulder out there and, as a result, each guy is able to hit only a very narrow section of the water. I found out later that the tension sometimes became so high on crowded nights that a fist fight occasionally broke out because of tangled lines and/or lost fish. Well, that kind of "close quarters" fishing is not for me, but on my first night out at the Point, I had to go with the flow. And so it was. I was astonished when all the fishermen who had arrived at Fishermen's Landing descended the cliff and set up shop right next to me — not 30 or 40 yards away, but close enough that I could have easily touched the two guys on either side of me with my fishing rod. And without so much as a hello, they just began casting. Then one of the guys leaned over and asked if I had caught anything. I remember thinking to myself; "The nerve of this guy — he practically climbs on my back to fish, and then he wants a fishing report as well?" But diplomacy prevailed and I told him that I had a few nice swirls, but no fish on. He said that he thought that was encouraging and went right back to casting.

I didn't notice immediately, but it soon became apparent to me that I was the only person who was using a popper. The rest of the guys were all using swimmers, most of which were needlefish of one color or another. I can't remember how long after those guys arrived before the first hookup, but it was an embarrassingly short time period compared with the amount of time I had been there casting the popper. It was one of the guys fishing right next to me who got the first fish. By that point, it was dark, and I wouldn't have known that he had a fish on except for the fact that he was standing so close to me — he never said a thing. But the bend in his rod told the whole story. This was a big fish and I could hear it peeling line from his reel. Instinctively, I retrieved my lure so that I wouldn't interfere with his catch, and then I stood in the darkness watching as he fought this fish. I couldn't help thinking that he had caught his fish right next to me, and right in the spot where I was casting. And then the light bulb went on — it was the popper — it had to be. Just then, the fisherman started backing up and pulling this huge silvery shadow into the shallow water where the small rocks were sticking out. He grabbed the leader and dragged it a little further until it was on solid ground. That's when I finally got a decent look at it. I couldn't believe my eyes. It was a huge beautiful female striper that was easily over 40 pounds. I had never seen anyone catch a bass this big before. It was simply enormous. I was so excited that I reached for my flashlight to shine it on the fish so I could get a better look at it. Suddenly I noticed that this guy was not nearly as excited as I was; he was getting more disturbed by the minute from all the attention I was giving his catch. Sensing that my adoration was less than desirable, I decided that I'd better go back to fishing. But when I turned around to return to my spot, another guy had moved in! I quickly found that the rule at the Point was "use it or lose it." I sat down on a log on the shore and figured that I'd watch and see if any more fish were landed. Sure enough, in about half an hour, several more large fish were beached by different fishermen, all on needlefish, and each time with its captor trying to be as secretive as possible regarding his catch. Very little light was used by each fisherman while he unhooked his catch, and the lights were never flashed around the beach or on the water.

I learned a lot that night. First and foremost that bass much prefer swimming plugs, like the needlefish, over a fast-moving popping plug on a dark night. I fished intermittently that evening, in between landings of fish by *other* fishermen and open spots in which to stand, but I never got so much as a bump from my popper while the guys around me were pulling in nice-sized bass with some regularity. It also became quite clear that there was an air of secrecy that prevailed among those who were catching the fish. The reality was that with the striped bass population dwindling, and decent catches becoming increasingly difficult to find, most veteran fishermen were going to great lengths to keep the location of their catches secret. I would come to find out later that some guys even buried their catches in the sand or hid their fish in the thick beach-rose bushes on the shoreline. That way, other fishermen passing by would have no idea that they were standing on a productive spot. It was also not unusual for fishermen to try and follow the trucks of other fishermen who had weighed in fish from the night before. I quickly learned that if you got into good fish at a particular spot, you should keep your mouth shut, get them back to the truck with as little attention as possible, and by all means, not to take them to the bait shop scale to be weighed unless you're prepared to lie about where you caught them — otherwise, you could pretty much count on having plenty of company at your spot the next night.

It took several years and many, many trips out to the island to learn where the best fishing spots were and how to get to them. And although I eventually discovered (contrary to my initial belief) that Block Islanders are genuine and endearing people, like anyone else, they don't like fishermen trampling all over their private properties. Unlike the island of Martha's

Vineyard, there are plenty of ways to access the great fishing spots on Block Island without parking on, or walking across, someone's yard. But I found that it was necessary to visit and fish these spots for the first time during the day because at night, it was pretty near impossible to determine where you were, let alone where to cast. One of the easiest spots to fish, and by far, one of the best and most overlooked, is "The Steps" next to the Southeast Lighthouse. The bluffs and shoreline at the southeast end of the island are some of the Block's most rugged terrain, and aside from a small stretch of beach at the bottom of The Steps, it really takes time and patience to understand where to and where not to cast. For instance, positioned about midway between The Steps and Lucky 7 Cove is a long stretch of algae- and kelp-embedded rocks. Anyone who has ever hit this seaweed with a plug knows that the odds of getting his plug back once the weeds grab it are slim and next to none. Nevertheless, this area offers some of the best fishing on the island for bass and I have always predicted that if anyone ever had a good shot at a 60-pounder, it's a fair bet that it might be taken there.

As a side note, walking up The Steps (all 150 plus or minus of them) with all of your equipment and in heavy waders is no picnic, but if you're carrying a fish, don't expect sympathy from anyone. Actually, somehow a nice fish seems to make the trip up a little less burdensome.

Almost everyone can remember his first *big* bass. I landed mine on Sandy Point at the North Light in the middle of the afternoon. On that day, not only did I land the biggest fish I had ever caught up to that point, but I also discovered a lure that changed my fishing from that day forward. This was several years after graduate school and I had already moved to, and was living in, Tampa, Florida — although distance didn't stop me from making frequent trips back to the Block, because once you get "Block Fever," you have it for life. I decided to try my luck at Sandy Point that afternoon after having no success at several other spots. It was mid-October, the sky was overcast and there was light fog surrounding the island. I drove out to Sandy Point and was delighted to find that I was the only one there. The water on the west side of the Point was rolling in with some great-looking surf so I began fishing on that side. After my first experience at Southwest Point, I had long since switched to using needlefish plugs — green, yellow and pink were the colors that seemed to work best for everyone. It didn't take but a single cast that afternoon and wham! I was on! It was a big bluefish, and then several more after that. I kept looking over my shoulder to see if anyone else was coming out, but no one had arrived yet. In about an hour's time, I had managed to catch and release four or five large blues and two small bass. In the process, however, I had lost the only two needlefish plugs that I had to two bluefish break-offs. I started fumbling around in my surf bag, looking for another swimmer of any kind, when I remembered that I had packed one of the large deep-running swimming lures that is frequently used in Florida for snook and grouper fishing. It was a red-and-white Mirrolure, a model 103MR. Trouble was, the plastic lip on the plug was too large and it would have caused the plug to dive far too deep. I almost put it back in the bag when, out of desperation, I decided to see if the lip on the lure could be reduced with the aid of a sharp knife — and it worked. I carved the lip down to the size of a fingernail and tied it on to the leader. I was back in action. I wasn't sure how well it was going to work, but at least it was a swimmer and not a popper. First cast — wham! Fish on. And this one turned out to be a nice 15-pound bass. I didn't give it much thought; I was just elated that I still had a swimmer to use. The next fish, however, hit the Mirrolure with a hard strike, and when I set the hook, the fish took off for the mainland. I had never before had a fish run like this; it just kept taking line to the point that I had to look down at the reel to see how much line was left. I knew that if it didn't stop soon, I was going to have to stop it and take a chance on breaking the line, so I tightened the drag a little more. Finally, the fish tired and came to a stop. I must have had 200 yards of line out in the water, but I started to fight the fish back into shore and after several more short runs, I got the fish onto the beach. I don't know which one of us was more exhausted, the fish or me. It's not that fighting the fish was so physically exhausting; it was the excitement of knowing that you've got a big fish on, and *not* knowing just how big it could be! Your muscles tense up, your heart races, and all you keep thinking is, "Oh baby.... don't lose this one!" Until that day, my biggest fish was only about 25 pounds — and this one weighed in at just over 37. It was the first big striper that I had ever caught and I will never forget the experience.

I'm pretty sure that's the day I became a Block Island fishing addict. It was almost 25 years ago and, since then, I have fished the island as often as I could and I've caught more stripers in its waters then one man should be entitled to in a lifetime, most of which were released to fight again.

**The first *large* striped bass that I had caught on Block Island. It weighed just over 37 pounds, and ironically the picture was taken on Jamestown, where I brought the fish back to show it off.**

As an interesting sidelight, one day quite a few years ago I arrived on the Block for two or three days of fishing. I had parked my truck on Water Street across from the Harborside Inn because I needed to visit the Seaside Market to buy some provisions for the next couple of days. As I walked up the sidewalk to the market, I spotted a picture in the display/bulletin board case that used to be situated on two posts out in front of a clothing shop called the Red Herring. It was a framed photograph of a guy fishing and standing (somewhat perilously) on a bunch of slime-covered boulders in the surf, while at the same time a huge wave had broken over the rocks which had made it appear as though it was a miracle that this fisherman could be able to stand there. It was an amazing photograph and I stopped to admire it before proceeding into the market. Malcolm Greenaway, one of New England's most accomplished photographers, had taken the picture from the top of the bluffs near the Southeast Lighthouse. The photograph is called "The Surfcaster" and a more appropriate picture for the cover of this book I couldn't imagine. It can still be seen (and purchased) today in Greenaway's gallery at the top of Water Street. I found out a few years ago that many people had inquired as to who the fisherman in the photo was — it's me.

# Chapter IV

## Harvey and Mike

I'm not sure, exactly, what year I met Harvey Waxman for the first time; however, I was already familiar with his Southwest Point house (inside and out) before we had ever met. Little did I know then that a great and lasting friendship would eventually develop between us. I used to fish Southwest Point a lot — sometimes all night long — without bothering to explore the fishing possibilities at other spots around the Block. And when you're down on the Point for that amount of time, you see a lot of folks come and go. Some are fishermen, and some are vacationers just down to walk the beach. One afternoon in late July, I was fishing the Point under cloud-covered skies and light fog. My daughter, Kristen, who was all of 8 years old at the time, was with me. We had come over to the island for a few days so I could show her where all the fishing stories came from and to introduce her to the island's majestic beauty. Kristen was excited to see the Block for the first time and even more excited that we were going to do it camping-style (for one night) by sleeping in the Jeep.

In those days, you could drive your 4X4 almost to the water's edge at Southwest Point. That made it very convenient for me to fish while she would be sleeping (unfortunately, you can't drive down to the Point any longer, and camping or sleeping in your car is now strictly prohibited anywhere on the island). That afternoon, Kristen was treasure hunting up on the beach while I was taking a few casts to see if there were any fish around. There is more debris that washes up on Southwest Point than anywhere else on the island. This most likely occurs because there are strong cross-currents that merge there, and consequently it's not uncommon after a big storm to find enough driftwood to build a small house, in addition to a variety of other unusual artifacts. That made treasure hunting quite attractive from the viewpoint of an 8-year-old. In fact, it wasn't long before Kristen had company in her quest for beach treasures. She was joined by another girl who had come down to the beach with her mom to do the very same thing. I didn't know it at the time, but their family had rented Harvey's house for the week and the other little girl was delighted to have found someone her own age to play with. Well, one thing led to another and (after ascertaining that these were respectable folks) Kristen spent the evening at Harvey's with her new friend while I fished through the night.

As I recall, it was a very good night for fishing. By morning, I had over a dozen large bluefish and a striper that was about 20 pounds. Although I'm not big on bluefish as table fare, Mary Shepley will eat just about anything with fins on it and she often repays favors from her neighbors with bluefish fillets. Since Kristen and I were staying with the Shepleys when we returned to Jamestown, all the fish were gutted and iced for later delivery. The next morning I went up to the house to get Kristen. I had a cup of coffee with her friend's grandparents and gave them a side fillet of striped bass for being so nice to her. Sitting there with my coffee, I remember looking out from the huge picture windows that face the ocean in the main room and thinking to myself what an incredible location the house was in. It sits high atop a 50-foot bluff, overlooking one of the best fishing spots on the entire island, and with a beautiful view of the eastern end of Long Island and Montauk Point in the distance. It would be such a luxury to be able to walk less than 100 yards to a great fishing spot whenever the urge hit you (knowing that your scotch and a warm bed were only a stone's throw away if the fish became uncooperative). Little did I know that I would soon have the privilege of experiencing such fishing bliss.

Given how much time I have spent fishing Southwest Point, it's no surprise that I would eventually run into Harvey. I think it was late one fall afternoon while I was taking a break from casting, sitting on one of the giant logs that so frequently wash up on the beach there. Harvey had come down to the beach with one of his sons to look things over and as he walked by, he made a remark about the unusual plug I was using. At the time — and for many years after that — I was the only one on the island who religiously used a Mirrolure. Several years before, and quite by accident, I had discovered what a remarkably effective lure it was for stripers (especially the red-and-white version). It is just plain deadly. Harvey said, “Hi,” and then asked what I was fishing with. I explained that it was a Mirrolure (similar to the type that I used on the Florida flats — except much larger) and that after many years of fishing for striped bass, I had never found anything more effective. Since Harvey was just beginning to learn the ins and outs of striper fishing, he was all ears and, of course, wanted to know where he could get some. I told him that they were not available in New England (at least not in any tackle shop that I’d ever been in), but that he was welcome to have one of my spares. I had no problem giving away a lure because the Mirrolure Company was giving them to me at cost in trade for any pictures of large stripers that I caught using them. After some conversation regarding what a nice fishing spot the Point was, Harvey explained that he owned the house directly overlooking it, and when I told him the story of already visiting his house with my daughter, we both had a good laugh.

In a way, Harvey is much like Raymond. They both share a tremendous interest in fishing, a great sense of humor, complete neglect of their fishing equipment (at least during the early years), and a propensity to suffer a seemingly disproportionate share of the consequences of Murphy's Law for Fishing. Harvey is also the intellect's intellect and a well-known psychologist. The time he doesn't spend fishing, he spends reading — which is, perhaps, why his fishing success in the early years was somewhat limited. On the other hand, there aren't many people with whom I enjoy engaging in conversation more than Harvey. We have solved many of the world's problems over a few glasses of Laphroaig (real fishermen's scotch), especially one afternoon when we decided to sample a variety of different bourbons in a sort of "bourbon taste-off" with one of Harvey's friends, Mike Levin — it was great fun at the start, but it ended up being an Excedrin event that I'm sure all of us would rather forget about.

During the next striper season following my first encounter with Harvey, I fished as often at Southwest Point as a guy from Tampa could — usually during the day on Saturdays and then for all of Saturday night before having to head back to the boat and then off to the airport. I became friends with Harvey and his family and I was frequently invited to stay with them when I came out to the island to fish. I was very appreciative of their hospitality and they were likewise appreciative of the striped bass fillets and the fishing advice. To many folks, traveling from Tampa to Block Island might seem like a strenuous undertaking just to catch stripers. But remember, in the early '80s there weren't a lot of bass around and the fact that the fish would show up at the Block on a fairly consistent basis was enough to justify, in my mind at least, that the rewards were well worth the trek. On many of the nights that I fished the Point during the early '80s, especially in the spring, I would never see another fisherman. This was in sharp contrast to the '70s, when a line of 15 to 20 fishermen, all jostling for a casting position, was a common sight.

After seeing that I was catching bass at the Point on a consistent basis, Harvey began to get far more serious about fishing as well. After all, these weren't the 50-pounders of the '70s, but there were plenty that were over the minimum size limit and most of those were in the 20-pound range. At first, Harvey made the same mistake that many beginners do — a few casts, no hits, give up. One thing that I've learned about fishing for stripers is that when you're in a spot that is known to consistently produce fish, you have to be patient. If you're lucky, you may find fish on your first cast. Usually, however, you have to cast for extended periods until a school of fish moves in or until the tide allows you to cast to just the right spot — or sometimes (and for no apparent reason) until the fish that were there the whole time suddenly decide it's time to put on the feedbag. This is especially true with the coastline around Block Island. I have concluded after many years of fishing the island's waters that, unless the fish have found a bait school and have managed to pin the school into a cove, the stripers are constantly moving in search of food. There are many nights when I have been casting for two or three hours without so much as a bump, and then all of a sudden, there they are, one after another, only to disappear shortly thereafter. On other nights, you may find the action to be on and off, and of course no matter how good you are, there are always some nights when you should have just plain gone to bed.

Initially, fishing with Harvey was of the "drive-by" style….. a few casts, no hits, and off he would go on his way back up to the house. I could see, however, that each time we fished together his interest in the sport was growing and his endurance was improving. One day, I asked him if he would like to join me and Lou, a former business partner, for a trip over to Black Rock later that evening. I had heard that there were some nice fish taken in that area the night before. Harvey agreed to go and so the three of us headed for the south shore after dinner that evening. It was the first week of June and the days were already fairly long. When we arrived at Black Rock, it was just starting to get dark but there was enough light remaining to allow us to position ourselves on rocks of our choosing and without using our flashlights. Lou had climbed far out onto a rock about a hundred yards down the shoreline from me. Harvey was positioned on a rock about halfway between us. The tide that evening must have been exceptionally low because each of us had to do some reasonable rock climbing in the surf in order to get out far enough and into a position where we could cast to open water. Fishing the south and southeastern shores of the Block can be some of the most difficult and challenging surf fishing anywhere in the Northeast. When I mention to fishermen in south Florida (who have never fished the New England coastline) that I surfcast for striped bass in New England, most of them contrive this vision of guys sitting on a sandy beach in their lounge chairs, beers in hand, and with surf rods comfortably positioned in sand spikes awaiting the fish to strike. The truth is that there aren't many other types of night fishing that are more rugged, physically challenging, and downright dangerous than striper fishing from the slick boulder fields of the Block Island surf. When it's pitch-black out there, and the surf is heavy, you really have to keep your wits about you.

Well, that evening at Black Rock was pitch-black dark all right, but the surf was as calm as a lake, which was quite unusual. When the surf is that smooth, you tend to become a little more adventurous and more willing to venture farther out on the rocks, especially with a low tide that was still receding. After quickly surveying the waterline, I decided to position myself in a spot that looked rather promising, but after a dozen or so casts, I started to eye a very large rock that was partially submerged about 15 yards in front of me. The tide was exceptionally low, but even so, this rock was way out there. Nevertheless, I wasn't catching anything so I decided that since the ocean was so invitingly calm, it might be worth the effort to slowly wade out into the surf and see if it was possible to reach the rock without going under. I remember the experience as if it happened yesterday. I was moving ever so slowly, slinking my way into the ocean in the blackness of the night, and knowing that one wrong step might have put me under. It was incredibly intimidating, and I didn't want to use my light for fear of spooking any fish that were in the vicinity. The water level the entire way out was within six inches of the top of my chest waders and once I had reached the rock, climbing up onto the top of it took every bit of strength I had left. Once on top, though, I suddenly gained a renewed sense of energy from this new casting perspective and the fishing prospects were suddenly looking ever so promising. So it was back to business as the first cast streaked out across the dark, silent water. It's amazing how fast the anxiety subsides with the possibility of a catch and the security of sound footing. And much to my surprise and satisfaction, my daunting journey out to the rock was nicely rewarded with a hookup on the very first cast. It felt like a fairly nice fish too, but for some reason I managed to lose it about halfway in. This happened again several more times and by then Harvey started wondering what was going on. Because the night was so silent due to the absence of breaking surf, he could hear the fish that I hooked splashing around (along with my unmentionable mutters of frustration) each time I set the hooks, but he couldn't see a thing in my direction. Harvey was still about 50 yards away and he hadn't had a hit yet. He shouted over to me to ask what was happening and I shouted back, "School! I think I'm in a school!" Now, although Lou was still about a hundred yards away from me and couldn't make out anything that I was saying, he could hear Harvey as well as I could because Harvey was in between us. When he shouted over to Harvey to ask what I was shouting about, Harvey shouted back, "He said something about being in a school" (the whole thing was rather comical). Well, Harvey may not have understood the implications of someone shouting "school," but let me tell you, Lou was off of his rock in seconds, flying down the shoreline as fast as the boulder field would allow on a pitch-black night. In the meantime, I had finally managed to land one of these bass — which was close to 15 pounds — and I figured that it would be prudent at this point to get off the rock and get the fish to shore before I lost it. The journey back to shore with the fish seemed like a cakewalk compared to the trip out. When I reached the shore, Lou was there waiting for me, anxious to get the details. I told him to go right out to the rock and take a few casts because there were fish at the end of every cast. I remember him saying, "Way out there?!" then, looking back at my fish and without giving it another thought, out he went. Within five minutes, he was on *his* way back with a bass of identical size. As you might have guessed, Harvey wasn't about to be left out of this action and although at first he may not have realized that I was into a mini-blitz, he was there ready to take his turn at navigating the English Channel as soon as Lou reached the shore. Once there, Harvey was also quick to enjoy the same success and returned to shore with his fish, again the same size as the first two.

So there we were, sitting on the shore, so overjoyed with our success that none of us even wanted to go back out to the rock and try for another fish. The limit that year was one keeper per person anyway, so we were just as happy to go back to the house, drink scotch, and congratulate each other over a fine evening — for in those lean years, it was indeed a fine evening when *everyone* got a keeper. I will always remember Harvey's comment as we sat in the Adirondack chairs that night, admiring the three handsome fish on the deck in front of us, looking out at the sea, and taking in the warm spring air as we sipped our Laphroaig…., "Damn, we're good," he mused, "limited out, and on the deck drinking scotch by 10:30!" A rare and pleasant occurrence, I assure you.

As a side note, the rock we fished from that night is still there today and in the same position that it was years ago, and I have to tell you that after seeing in the daylight how far out into the surf we'd journeyed, I thought it nothing short of a miracle that we all made it back to shore to once more sip amber liquid.

**Harvey Waxman and me with three nice bass after risking our necks to reach them.**

Mike Levin is one of Harvey's best friends and a very talented and highly respected physician. Several years after Harvey and I had become good friends, Harvey invited some of his friends out to the island to join my group for a few days of fishing. When the guys in my group met Mike for the first time, we all agreed that he was one of the most likable guys you would ever want to meet. We also quickly discovered that just when we thought that there couldn't be anyone with worse luck than Raymond, with more equipment problems than Harvey, and at greater risk of falling into the water on a consistent basis than all of us put together, along comes Mike. Mike's propensity to catch seaweed (big clumps of it — he didn't fool around with the little stuff) and large rocks is surpassed only by his affinity for the water, it not being uncommon for him to take an unscheduled swim now and then (not that the rest of us haven't been familiar with an unexpected dip in the surf, it's just that Mike did it with stunning regularity). But even though Mike was sometimes awkward in his approach, he was equally as determined to catch fish. Unfortunately, on many occasions, determination was all that Mike had going for him.

A classic example of this was the day that Harvey, Mike, and I went to fish Black Rock one fall afternoon. Harvey decided to head down the beach to the far corner of the cove we had selected and Mike and I went the other way to fish the opposite corner. As it turned out, Mike and I made a lucky decision. I climbed out on the rocks in the corner of the cove to position myself as far out into the water as possible without being in danger of getting knocked off by an incoming breaker. Mike was a little more cautious and stayed on shore as we began to cast. I was immediately onto a fish as soon as my lure hit the water. It was a small bass and I released it only to catch two or three more fish of the same size. Meanwhile, Mike still hadn't had a hit. I looked back over my shoulder to try to figure out why Mike wasn't getting hookups because the fish were clearly out there, and apparently in good numbers. I soon realized that from where Mike was casting, he wasn't able to reach the spot where the bass were concentrated, so I pointed to a nice flat rock about 10 yards in front of him and beckoned to him to wade out to it and cast. He did so, and was onto a fish on the very next cast. Now for Mike, a fish on was a serious event. Heretofore, Mike's success had been somewhat limited, to put it mildly, so Mike wasn't about to lose an opportunity to bolster his record (or start one — I don't think he had caught his first keeper bass at that point), so he decided that while fighting this fish, it would be prudent to start backing his way into shore. The problem was that he forgot that he was standing on a rock that was two feet above the waterline so as he proceeded back without looking, he fell backwards off the rock. I had managed to turn around at just that moment. I remember seeing him disappear into the surf and then, to my amazement, I could see that even though he was underwater, his hands were sticking out of the surf and were still firmly attached to the rod while he continued reeling and fighting this fish! A few seconds later, he emerged from the suds only to be knocked down to one knee by an incoming breaker — again, all the while fighting the fish. What I didn't know until later was that during the fall, Mike landed against another submerged rock and sustained a muscle injury that took more than a few weeks to heal. Nonetheless, he landed that fish as if it were a 50-pound trophy. When I had to tell him that it was too short to keep….. well, you can just imagine. From that day forward, no matter how awkward Mike may have been in his approach, he won my respect for his grit and determination — and the invitation to fish with me any day.

No matter how good (or lucky) a fisherman you may be, there will always be a few days in your fishing log book that you wish you could forget. Such was the case one fall morning about a year later when I was fishing with Harvey and Mike and some of the others in our group.

It was the next morning following an afternoon in October when Max and I had lucked into a small blitz of nice bass down at Black Rock. Max Fahnestock was a former AT&T client of mine. Max has been an avid hunter and fisherman for most of his life. He had joined our fishing group in the early '90s and has been an integral and cherished member of our gang ever since. Max and I were out on the Block early, ahead of the rest of the group, to set up the house that we had rented for the week. We came back to the house from Black Rock with four nice bass, the largest being about 42 pounds. The rest of the guys arrived later that evening and the chatter during dinner was understandably optimistic about what the next morning's fishing prospects might hold for us. The house that we had rented was large, as it had to accommodate eight fishermen, and it was located out on Southwest Point within several hundred yards of Harvey's place. Harvey and Mike were the last of the group to arrive that evening and they came over to our house for cocktails and a fishing report before turning in for the night. When they saw the excellent catch that Max and I had managed to score, their level of enthusiasm was heightened considerably, and further bolstered by the weather report, which forecast a warm front with light rain to arrive early the next morning. Warm fronts with overcast conditions and modest winds can be the harbinger of some very good daytime fishing — especially in October. This one was to be no exception.

Before heading back to his house with Mike, Harvey asked me what time we would all be heading out to fish the next morning (we were all too exhausted to go out and fish that night). I told him that we should plan on getting to Black Rock by 5 a.m. and that we would meet them there around that time. When Bruce, Max, and I woke up the next morning, we were running a little behind schedule and it was already starting to get light outside, enough so that we could see that Harvey and Mike had already left and that we needed to get a move on. The weather forecasters were on the money with their prediction; we were greeted with an overcast sky and light rain. When we reached the dirt access road out to Black Rock, it was already very muddy and full of large puddles that appeared ominously deep for anything other than a four-wheel-drive vehicle. We arrived at the Black Rock parking area and sure enough, Harvey's Suburban was already there. It looked as if he and Mike had already descended the cliff and had proceeded to fish the spot where Max and I had success the day before. However, when Max, Bruce, and I had descended the bluff-head down to the surf, Harvey and Mike were nowhere to be found. Although the three of us thought this to be a little unusual, we could hear the bass calling our names from the surf, so the whereabouts of Harvey and Mike was not the pressing issue of the moment.

The surf on this fine cloudy October morning was really humming, with lots of beautiful whitewater cascading toward the shoreline as far as you could see in every direction. The tide had another hour before it would reach the high water mark and the conditions just seemed to have fish written all over them. The three of us picked out rocks in the surf to cast from, separated by about 30 yards from each other. As I climbed up on my rock, I glanced down the coastline and noticed what appeared to be two other surf fishermen very far off in the distance — Harvey and Mike. They had arrived so far ahead of us that they had been able to fish the coastline a mile beyond where we were standing. Suddenly, my attention was drawn to the fact that Bruce was already onto his first fish. Likewise, my first cast took a strike and I was onto a fish as well. I couldn't see Max from where I was standing, but I remember hearing a few minutes later over the radio (we all carried small hand-held radios for safety and general communication) that he was onto a fish as well. Sure enough, like the afternoon before, the fish were still in this area, and although they were not huge (most in the 15-to-20-pound range), they were constant. The hookups continued for at least the next half-hour. Finally spotting this action as they began to work their way back toward us, Harvey and Mike picked up their pace. By this time, Bruce and I had each landed and released at least a half-dozen small bass and we each had one nice keeper on the shore behind us. When Harvey got within earshot, I asked if they had taken any fish and I received a somewhat disgruntled negative response. No matter, the fish were right in front of us and they were still going strong. During the next 10 minutes or so, I caught and released another small fish and then hooked into what I thought was a very large bass. The bend in my rod was significantly greater than that from any of the other fish so far, and although the fish was not running line off the reel, the resistance was considerable. Just about that time, Harvey, feeling somewhat frustrated, had positioned himself within about 15 feet of where I was standing, and began to cast, thinking that it would be a no-lose proposition. He was probably correct, but when he attempted to cast his lure, the bail on his reel apparently closed prematurely, breaking his line with a crisp snap and sending his plug halfway to Montauk — never to be seen again. Meanwhile, I had discovered that the fish that I was fighting was not a huge fish after all; it was a small fish that, in the process of thrashing around, had managed to hook itself in the tail with the rear treble hook. The front treble hook that was originally in the bass' mouth had dislodged and as a consequence, I was pulling this fish in *by its tail* — in front of Harvey, who was frantically trying to re-rig his rod. It was quite clear that this did absolutely nothing to temper the level of his frustration. Sensing this, I quickly released the fish and climbed back onto my rock to cast, noticing that Bruce had just received a hit and, with a quick set of the hooks, was onto another fish. By this time, Harvey had re-rigged his rod with a new lure and was on his way down to the water's edge to cast. I turned to watch as he swung the rod forward with a very determined, sweeping and powerful back-cast. Well, this time the snap of his line was loud enough that it even got Bruce's attention. Another lure, on its way to Montauk. To make matters worse, Mike had moved into a position near where Harvey was standing and appeared to be onto a nice fish. The look of disgust was so poignantly painted over Harvey's face, that I wasn't sure that I wanted him to see me get another hookup — at least not yet. So, back up on the rocks, away from the surf, to attach another lure went Harvey. Mike was battling a fish, Bruce had just landed a fish — this one a keeper — and I went back to casting. Suddenly it occurred to me that Mike had been fighting his fish for some time now and judging from the angle of the line, it appeared that the fish was in the rocks fairly close to shore. At just that moment, however, my attention was diverted by a nice hit, and I was onto a fish once again.

Now what I didn't realize, is that prior to our arrival that morning, the day had already started out on a sour note for Harvey and Mike, and the residual aggravation from the morning's earlier incident was not helping Harvey's mood whatsoever. On the way out to the Black Rock parking area, and in an effort to avoid a large rock on the muddy dirt road, Harvey's Suburban had slid sideways into a water-filled pothole and a large rock protruding from the dirt wall of the very narrow roadway had taken out both side-panels of his vehicle. I'm glad I wasn't there to see that.

Well, this time, when Harvey came down to the water's edge to cast, all eyes were upon him and everyone was thinking, "No way — it couldn't possibly happen again." But sure enough, as the third time is so often the charmer, it was anything but that on this day. For the third time in a row, a sharp snap pierced the sound of the rolling surf as yet another shiny new Mirrolure was on its way to Montauk. As you might imagine, this was just too much to take. Poor Harvey. Everyone around him was catching fish — and Harvey couldn't even get a lure into the water — at least not one attached to his rod. In a rage most fitting and appropriate for the moment, Harvey stomped up the beach from the waterline and with one long, sweeping motion, hurled his surf rod as hard and as far as he could throw it. If it had been an Olympic event, he would've won. The rod left his hand, spinning in sideways circles from tip to butt several times until it hit the unforgiving rocks at the base of the cliff. Bruce and I figured that at this point, it was a good time to go back to fishing and make like we didn't notice. When I turned around to cast, I couldn't believe my eyes — Mike was still fighting his fish! However, upon further study, I realized that Mike had hooked into some of the kelp-like algae attached to a large rock (his specialty) that was about 10 yards out in front of him. Every time a wave came in, the algae would move a few feet toward the shore, which made Mike think he was gaining on this imaginary fish, and every time the water receded, the algae would pull back, taking line from his drag, and presumably making it feel as if the "fish" was "fighting back." I finally had to break the news to him which he received relatively well, because this rock had literally worn him out. I remember seeing Harvey and Mike leave shortly after that — Harvey grumbled a "See ya" as they both headed toward the path up the cliff, carrying the remains of Harvey's surf rod, which had reel parts, dirt, and other stuff hanging down from it. I guess some days are just better than others, and then there are other days..... well, you know.

Max, Bruce, and I quit fishing later that morning and returned to the rental house with two nice bass each — it had been quite a morning. To Harvey's credit, after he and Mike arrived back at his house, Harvey picked up a spare rod and went right back out into the surf at Southwest Point, where he was finally rewarded with a keeper bass, and which I assure you, elevated his spirit immensely. Later that day, we all got back together for cocktails and stories. With Harvey now far more receptive to discussion, we asked him to explain the new sport he created that morning — the "rod toss." He simply smiled and said: "Hey, they throw golf clubs and tennis rackets, don't they?"

Just as there are days you wish to forget, there are those to remember forever......

I was in my office and on a conference call the morning the call came in from Harvey. My secretary put a note in front of me that read: "Harvey Waxman called. All he said to tell you was '49 pounds' — and that you'd know what that meant."

Indeed I did. It was the second week of July and Harvey had been out at his place on the Block for the weekend. As he explained it to me, he intended to go out and fish the Point below his house on the evening he had arrived. However, after dinner and a few scotches, the comfort of his easy chair got the best of him and he fell asleep. He awoke the next morning, around 6 a.m., and, realizing that his fishing opportunities were quickly diminishing, grabbed his rod and headed down the path to the Point. When he arrived at the shoreline, there were four guys present who had been fishing all night without any success whatsoever. Hearing the discouraging news, Harvey decided to take a few casts anyway, and on his third cast, he took a tremendous hit and was onto a fish. The four fishermen were stunned, but when they saw this fish come in, *all 49 pounds of it*, I'm sure the look of disbelief must have stayed on their faces for a week. Here they had fished all night long without catching a thing and along comes Harvey, and nonchalantly lands a trophy striper within three casts! To rub salt into the wound, Harvey asked the guys to watch his fish while he went back up to the house to get a wheelbarrow because the fish was too heavy to carry. They agreed with some very stiff smiles and then immediately went back to casting, but to no avail —

no more fish were caught that morning — a morning to remember forever (or forget, depending upon your perspective)!

**Mike Levin with a handsome striper that was well deserved in consideration of the dues that Mike had paid in the past.**

**The author with his two fish and Bruce's two fish after everyone else had departed on the morning of the famous "rod toss."**

# Chapter V

## The Perfect Storm, Understanding the Conditions & Common Sense

One of the primary forces that exerts an ever-changing effect on the quality of fishing at any given point in time is, of course, the weather. Weather conditions have been responsible for creating some of the most incredible fishing I've ever experienced and, alternatively, some of the worst. On an island, the effects of wind and other elements are more intense than on the mainland and are always the subject of scrutiny by knowledgeable fishermen. The key elements in the weather package that have the greatest influence on the quality of fishing (and to a great extent, whether or not you *can* fish), are the wind and the barometric pressure.

It used to be that when I would leave the office in Tampa en route to an extended fishing trip out to the Block, my office colleagues who didn't fish would remark, "Have a good time; hope the weather's great!" My response would always be: "Thanks, but please don't wish for good weather." Of course, I would get a puzzled stare until I explained that generally, inclement weather improves the fishing. Now everyone in the office knows better and the farewell is more likely to be, "Hope the weather sucks while you're out there."

For fishing, I can't imagine any forecast I'd rather hear than cloudy with periods of light rain, and a wind at 10 to 15 knots coming from any direction that has the word "south" in it. A 15-knot fresh breeze just seems to have a magical effect on enhancing the willingness of the fish to bite, although the wind direction can be equally important as speed. I prefer a wind from the southeast, south or southwest. The reason is simply that after tracking my fishing successes over the past 30 years, the evidence shows that the best striped bass fishing I've experienced has occurred during nights (and days) when the wind direction had a southern element to it. An occasional exception is an east or northeast wind. I don't think there's any mystery to this pattern; it's just that inclement weather usually comes in on the heels of northeastern and southerly wind directions — especially with the nor'easters. And fronts that come in on southerly wind directions usually bring warmer and more comfortable fishing conditions as well, even though they also have a tendency to be very wet.

Enter the aspect of barometric pressure here. It's no secret that rain and otherwise "snotty" weather usually accompanies low barometric pressure, and when the barometer begins to fall, fishing usually begins to improve. On the other hand, a rising barometer seems to have completely the opposite effect, shutting down the bite and signaling the onset of approaching fair weather. Now if the barometric pressure is high, it's a pretty fair bet that you've got west, northwest, or north wind. I can tell you without hesitation that a north or northwest wind forecast is usually a harbinger of bad news for the fishing scene. Of course, there are no absolutes in fishing or in weather and I'm sure there are plenty of veteran fishermen who will read this and then remember that they had some great striper days on north or northwest winds, but if you consider your total experiences over the years, I think you'll agree with me.

Now there's a fine line between the right amount of wind for great fishing and too much of a good thing. Sooner or later, it's directly related to the amount of suspended material that eventually clouds the surf if the wind is too strong for too long. There's a big difference between raging surf and raging surf with dirty water — you just won't catch many fish in the latter. One of the first things that my group does when we arrive on Jamestown or the Block is a scouting run around the island to determine which spots have potential. The most important factors that we look for, in addition to diving birds and fish busting bait, is water clarity — in other words, how much suspended material (i.e. sand, floating weed, etc.) is in the water. Since for many years now everyone in my group has fished exclusively with lures, water clarity is directly related to our chances for success (simply put, a fish isn't going to strike at something it can't see). Huge breakers caused by strong winds can churn up so much suspended sand, clay and weed into the surf that the suspended material makes it virtually impossible for a fish to see your plug. And my guess is that the fish don't frequent this kind of environment for very long because they probably aren't thrilled at having all that stuff go through their gills.

This situation frequently occurs on Block Island's south shore. The south shore is one of my favorite fishing spots on the island, especially below the Southeast Lighthouse and along the entire Black Rock area. But when it rains very hard for extended periods, the clay from the exposed bluffs along the southern shoreline will wash down into the water, giving the water the appearance of a chocolate milkshake.

I was fishing at Black Rock on a spring afternoon a couple of years ago and the fishing action was red-hot. Raymond and I were fishing in what we've named the "Cove of Plenty," and several others in our group were fishing in the next cove over. When we arrived at Black Rock, it was about 1:30 in the afternoon. The wind was blowing about 15 knots out of the southwest and it was heavily overcast. A front had been forecast to pass through that afternoon and it looked as if it was going to pour at any moment. Raymond and I started catching fish right off the bat, and the action was steady, with a fish on about every three or four casts. Since most of us carry waterproof radios these days, Jim and Debbie radioed in that they were having the same success in the next cove over. The fish, they said, weren't large; in fact, most were just under the Rhode Island legal minimum at the time, but the action was great. I don't think we had fished for more than half an hour before the heavens opened up with a rain deluge. Since this was June, my immediate concern was lightening, but luckily there wasn't any so we kept fishing. With the rain now coming down as a heavy downpour, the fishing action intensified even further. We were hitting stripers on almost every cast when I turned around and noticed that it had been raining so hard, the clay was starting to wash down from the bluffs and into the water. We kept fishing, but it didn't take more than 15 minutes before the opaque clay/water combination extended out into the surf, almost to half our casting distance. I couldn't believe it! I knew what was about to happen, but I had never actually observed the process developing right in front of me, and at such a tremendous pace. Jim and Debbie radioed in, claiming that the same thing was happening in front of them, and all the way down the south shore as far as they could see. I radioed back and told them to kiss the fishing goodbye. Sure enough, as soon as the clay immersion line reached beyond our casting distance, the bite turned off as if someone had thrown a giant switch — fishing over.

Depending upon the tides and how long and hard it rains, the surf will usually return to normal in about two or three days. However, in a big storm, sometimes the entire island becomes encircled with a ring of clay that gives the water the appearance of a chocolate milkshake and it may take a week or more for the water to clear. This problem doesn't happen nearly as often in the waters around Jamestown because there the bluffs are mostly solid rock, not clay. Nevertheless, following a large storm, the surf just about everywhere becomes "garbaged up," sending surfcasters in search of cleaner waters or back home to work on their tackle.

I can speak with some authority about fishing in tough conditions with strong wind, intense rain, and big surf. I was one of the few (and foolish) fishermen out on the Block during the entire duration of The Perfect Storm during the last week of October 1991. What an incredible experience that was! I was staying at Harvey's on Southwest Point with Bruce, Raymond, Bill, and Bill's brother, Jim Shepley. We had planed to fish the island for the whole week. Two days after we arrived, however, the wind picked up considerably — and the forecast was for the wind to become even stronger yet. At first, we all figured what the hell? We had fished tough wind before. It was just a matter of finding the lee spots on the island. That was a good plan until the wind started whistling above 35 knots. The pork-chop shape of Block Island is such that, once it blows over 30 knots, the wind will do some very contrary-to-common-sense things, and over 40 knots, you're not likely to find a lee anywhere on the island. This happens primarily because the island just isn't big enough to front a shield against heavy wind. Strong winds will instead wrap around the corners of the pork chop, spoiling the spots where you would, by all reasonable expectation, think there to be a lee.

During our second afternoon on the island, when the National Weather Service forecast for Block Island Sound came over the weather radio predicting an extended period of 40- to 50-knot winds, the guys decided to give up and head back to the mainland. We still had no idea of the intensity of the storm that was about to materialize and I'm not sure the forecasters did either. Meanwhile, Bill had called to see when the next boat for the mainland would be leaving the island and he came back into the room to deliver the bad news. The boats had stopped running because the seas were too high (actually, the boats had stopped running that morning and didn't resume again for another five days, one of the longest cancellation periods ever). Since I had flown in from Tampa, I decided to stay on the island and see what the storm would bring. Besides, I had the truck, which left me with no alternative but to stay. The rest of the guys decided to try to catch a flight off the island if the planes were still flying. Luckily, they managed to get on the last plane to fly off the island for several days. And by the way, I was very happy *not* to be on that flight, which took off in a steady and snapping 50-knot wind! I remember seeing Bruce clawing at the window from inside the plane as it taxied away from the small terminal - somewhat in jest, but probably thinking to himself that it might not be such a bad idea to stay on the island after all.

What followed was the most incredible coastal storm I have ever seen. I will never forget going back into town for some provisions after I dropped the guys off at the airport and looking up at the flag on top of the National Hotel. The American flag was straight out and snapping sharply in the wind and the flagpole was oscillating back and forth with a precarious bend. I don't know if the wind finally ripped the flag off, but it was gone the next day and I doubt that anyone was foolish enough to climb up there to take it down. Actually, I was surprised that the flagpole was even there the next day.

With the other guys now off the island, and with a good supply of food, beer, and scotch to take back to the house, I decided to do a little scouting to see what effect the storm was starting to have on the island. It hadn't started to rain yet, but I figured that the wind would make for some pretty incredible surf, so I headed out to Black Rock to see what I could see. As I approached the small parking area out there, I was surprised that there were already about a dozen cars parked there ahead of me. I immediately thought to myself; "Wow, the fish must be in, big-time!" We fishermen are such great optimists. What was actually happening was quite to the contrary.

As I approached the cliff, I quickly saw the focus of everyone's attention. A very large fishing vessel of the dragger type had gone aground and was being hammered by 20-foot swells. The story, as I heard it from those who had been listening to their marine radios, was that the captain deliberately ran the ship aground to save his crew. Apparently the ship began taking on serious amounts of water through a faulty repair job to the hull, so much so that the boat lowered in the water as the large swells started breaking over the deck. Seeing this, the captain ran it hard into the rocky surf at Black Rock and told the crew to jump overboard and swim for their lives. As far as I know, everyone, including the captain, made it safely to shore. The ship, on the other hand, was another story.

I had never before experienced the destruction of such a large vessel by an angry ocean. At first, the 20-foot breakers were smashing into the ship, which had turned broadside, and its outriggers and radar equipment were being torn off and twisted like soft copper wire. The surf was so powerful that it eventually broke the ship in two and tossed it up on the beach like a Matchbox toy.

I came back the next day (after the storm had intensified even further that evening) to see what might be left of the ship. Much to my amazement, the back portion of the ship's deck from the mast to the stern was thrown far up onto the beach by the high tide and it was lying there relatively intact. The rest of the vessel had been completely destroyed and torn into small pieces that were scattered along the entire south side of the island, and as far away as Southwest Point. In fact, one of the several hundred-gallon fuel tanks ended up there, empty, and high up on the beach! To this day, if you look closely at the beach to the left of the Black Rock parking area, you can still see the diminished remnants of the ship's mast protruding from the sand on the beach. It stands as a potent reminder of the ocean's unpredictable and incredible power.

The second and third days of The Perfect Storm were the worst. The wind howled relentlessly at a constant 40 to 50 knots and peaked at gusts that were much higher. Rain squall-lines pounded the island with sheets of stinging rain all day long and then the storm's fury intensified even further during the second night. Back at Harvey's house, I had finished dinner and couldn't help but be captivated by the wind and rain that was furiously hammering the sides of the house. Harvey had installed some very nice weather instruments and the anemometer was being severely tested. I remember that just before the late evening news was about to air that night, the wind was gusting to 85 m.p.h.! And it was a good thing that the wind was coming from the northeast, because I'm not sure that the ten-foot high picture windows on the southwest side of the house would have survived a direct southwest wind coupled with the buckets of rain that were pounding the other side of the house at that point. Besides the wind and rain, there was a low, intermittent rumbling vibration that could be felt throughout the house being caused by the huge breakers crashing below the 50-foot bluff in front of the house. Some of the waves were easily 30 feet high and those off shore had to be bigger than that. I thought about how the weather prognosticators had missed their predictions, billing this as a two-day rain event with high wind. Until it was too late, no one had expected a hurricane-like storm that would last for almost five days.

It didn't take an expert to realize that the fishing scene around the entire island would be gone for many days to come. Even once the wind subsided, there would be so much dirt and debris in the water that it would take at least a week for things to get back to normal. Nevertheless, my curiosity to see what the storm had done to the island had me out the door early the next morning. The wind and rain were still pounding away at the island, but at least there was daylight so you could see what was going on. I headed downtown to Old Harbor, where the storm surge and high tide had pushed the water up and over the docks, flooding most of the parking lot and the ferry office. The seagulls were all standing on the ground facing into the wind (you know it's a bad storm when the gulls don't want to fly). Several boat owners were struggling to keep their boats attached to the pilings that were so submerged by the high water level they were having trouble containing the boats. One of the storm's striking exclamation points could be seen in the background. As you peered across the harbor, there were 25- to 30-foot swells that were smashing ferociously against the breakwater, sending thousand-gallon plumes of sea water 60 feet skyward. Not only was this a remarkable display of raw power, but you could actually feel the monster waves shake the ground as they hit that wall!

Needless to say, the island streets were a mess, cluttered with leaves, broken branches, and all sorts of debris. At northernmost point of the island, the waves had crashed over the end of Corn Neck Road and washed away a good bit of the asphalt while also spewing thousands of gallons of saltwater into Sachem Pond. Before going back to the house, I decided that it might be interesting to check out the view from the Southeast Lighthouse, but upon arriving at the Shit Chute (that's really what it's called) just below the Spring House, I found that the breakers were so big they were crashing all the way up the 50-foot bluff below the road. Part of the road had been washed away, and the remaining section was looking perilously unsafe. In fact, every now and then the top of a huge wave would be blown over the road by the wind. If you are familiar with this area below the Spring House, you know just how big those waves had to be to reach the road. Without much hesitation, I turned around for an alternate route back to the house.

During the afternoon of the third day, the rain finally ended, but the wind was still at a stiff and constant 40 knots. I resigned myself to reading in a comfortable chair back at the house accompanied by a liberal amount of amber liquid. The story wouldn't be complete, however, without revealing that fish were indeed caught the next day. I had discovered that, quite remarkably, the water in the Coast Guard Channel and in Great Salt Pond had managed to stay perfectly clean during the entire storm. Seeing this, but not really expecting to catch anything (and out of sheer boredom), I decided to take a few casts along the channel and into the pond. To my surprise, I was rewarded with a beautiful 10-pound bluefish and a handsome 34-inch striper. The fish weren't very big, but after four days of not being able to fish, they were trophies of the storm for which dues had been paid.

Speaking of paying your dues, which all fishermen have to do sooner or later, it comes to mind that not always are your dues paid by not catching fish. Long before witnessing the power and fury of The Perfect Storm, I was introduced, albeit unwillingly, to the might of the sea and the astonishing slickness of the algae that covers the rocks on her shoreline. We fisherman are a funny bunch sometimes. Guys fishing from the shore will sacrifice life and limb to crawl out to the farthest rock and perch themselves precariously in harm's way in order to add an extra 10 feet to the end of their cast. Meanwhile, the guys fishing from small boats will often nudge their bows into the shoreline, bouncing the boat off of submerged rocks, and ending up casting farther into shore than where the guys on the rocks are standing! Go figure — the grass is always greener, huh? But I'm no exception. My fishing colleagues will tell you that I used to climb the slick rocks like a fearless cat — what they don't know is that this cat has used up a few of his nine lives before instituting a more common-sense approach and learning to respect the power of the surf.

When I first started to seriously fish from New England's rocky shorelines, no one that I knew wore neoprene waders. We all had rubber or canvas chest waders and we knew that if we fell in and the waders filled up with water, it was practically the equivalent of having a cement block tied around your feet. For that reason, a wader belt was supposed to be worn tightly around the waist on the outside of the waders. That way, if you fell in, you'd have a chance to swim to safety — or so the theory goes. Such was not the case, sadly, for one of the best fishermen to ever fish Block Island.

**Ben Lubell — one of the best fishermen to fish the Block, who drowned, pulled in by the dangerous riptide off Sandy Point.**

On August 23, 1980, Ben Lubell and several of his friends were out fishing Sandy Point at the North Light. Ben was wearing his chest waders and standing waist-deep in the rip on the Point when he apparently stepped into an underwater hole and went down. The strong current swept him off the bar and his waders filled up with water, dragging him under. Bud Henshaw, an old-timer whom I met out on the island several years ago while fishing, told me that he was there the day it happened. He said everyone just felt helpless. One of the guys tried casting out to Ben, and another guy, who was not wearing waders, dove in to get Ben and actually had him for a brief moment, holding him by the back of his hood. But the current was too strong and he lost his grip. Meanwhile, the other fisherman was also swept off the Point and out to sea and had to be rescued by a passing boat. Bud said that when Ben's wife was told of the tragedy hours later, she asked if Ben had his waders on when he went under. Upon hearing the reply, she just bowed her head and walked away. Ben's body was recovered a week later from Cow Cove.

The rip at Sandy Point is no place for beginners. Breakers come across the sand bar from two different directions and, if you're not careful, the cross-current can easily take your feet out from under you. Once you're down, you're in trouble, because there's no way to stop yourself from being swept off the bar and into deep water. Ben was no beginner. He had been coming out to the island every summer to fish for over 26 years and he was one of the best and most experienced fishermen on the Block. A schoolteacher from New York, he was as passionate about fishing as he was about his profession, and everyone who knew him had only good things to say about him. I know how something like this can happen, even to an experienced fisherman. In my earlier years, I have been swept off rocks into heavy surf on two separate occasions. In each case, had it not been for a last-ditch effort to grab onto the rock where I was standing as the receding breaker was pulling me into deeper water, I might be fishing with Ben today.

I'm much more careful about which rock I decide to perch myself on these days, and after hearing what happened to Ben Lubell, most guys are far more careful about how far they step out into the rip on the Point. We also have better equipment available to us today, and if you fish alone at night as I often do, it's a good idea to invest in some of the basics. Korkers, for example, have been around for years. They're slip-on soles that fit over your wader boot and are then strapped on in various places around the boot. The bottoms have a network of short carbide steel spikes similar to the spikes on studded snow tires. The difference in stability when standing on slime-covered rocks with these things is just incredible! For a long time, I resisted wearing them because they were awkward, heavy, and took forever to put on and take off. Now, however, L.L.Bean sells a terrific lightweight adaptation called Stream Cleats, and that I highly recommend. You can carry them on your surf belt and slip them on and off in seconds. They're not for beach fishing, but for the rocks of the Block, they're indispensable. Another piece of equipment that might just save your life someday is an inflatable vest. The vests are made so small and lightweight these days that you hardly know you're wearing one. The vest is inflated with an enclosed $CO_2$ cartridge from a pull-cord on the front of the jacket. I started to wear one of these quite a few years ago whenever the surf conditions became really rough. They were fairly expensive then, but you can purchase one for a reasonable price these days. Neoprene is also a very buoyant material and it is generally thought that wearing neoprene waders is in itself a safety feature. I'm not sure this is actually true, and most manufacturers recommend that you do not rely on neoprene waders as a flotation device. Unless you use waders with 5mm neoprene thickness (3mm is the standard in New England for surf fishing), the weight of the boot foot filled with water could negate any buoyant effect the neoprene might have. Besides, fishing with neoprene waders in the spring, summer, and early fall can frequently be very warm and uncomfortable.

Finally, common sense just might be the best piece of equipment you don't have to buy. Eventually, everyone pays his dues — a hook in the finger, a fall off of slime-covered rocks, a rogue wave over your head, soaking you to the bone, a hand impaled by the excruciatingly sharp dorsal fin of a striper, hooking your waders with your own plug, and of course, casting your plug on the farthest cast it will ever make..... because you forgot to open the bail on your reel — been there, done them all. But with a little common sense *and* respect for the ocean, chances are that you'll be musing over paying your dues while more frequently lamenting your success stories in front of the fireplace with a nice cigar — amber liquid in hand, of course.

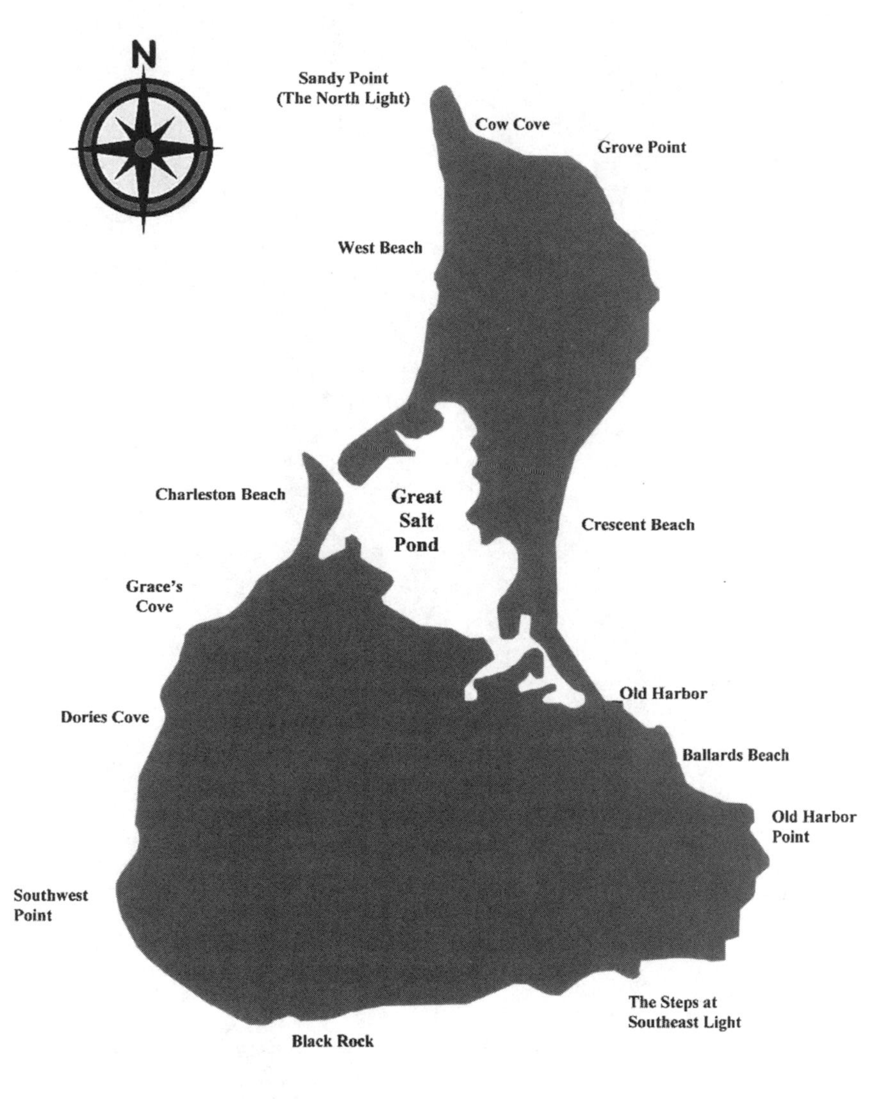


**Block Island**

CREEK BAIT SHOP
LEAD

# Chapter VI

## The Bait & Tackle Shop

### *Monarchs of the Island*

**B**ait and tackle shops are the watchdogs of the island fishing scene — sort of the central command for fishing expeditions. There is no place on the islands (although local bars are a close second) where more information can be found regarding what's biting, where the fish are (or were yesterday), who caught what and when, what bait or plug was used — you name it, there isn't much that goes on around a small island that doesn't eventually filter into one of the shops. The bait shop proprietors are the ministers of fishing information, and if you're not in their good graces, well, you'd better be dammed good at finding fish and hope that you don't need any additional bait, tackle, or equipment repairs on short notice. Similar to how barbershops used to be the place where guys hung out to get the latest town news, the bait shop is the listening post for the islands' coastal affairs. To a dedicated fisherman, a well-stocked tackle shop is the candy store for big boys and girls. It has always been difficult for me to drive by one of the shops without feeling compelled to stop in, check out the fishing news, and examine the tackle and other equipment I've already seen a hundred times before. I guess if you can't actually *be* fishing, the next best thing is to speak fishing, and have lots of fishing stuff around you.

Most fishermen never consider what the view is like from behind the bait shop counter, but it's a variety show *extraordinaire* to be sure. Every day, from April to November, the proprietor greets many fishermen, most with the same objective and most starving for up-to-date fishing reports and news. There are the pros who come into the shop and know exactly what they want. They don't ask for advice, and they don't give out any secrets either. Then there are the "ginkers" — the fishermen wannabes — who come in and buy every piece of equipment under the sun, but haven't a clue how to use it, and never ask. And then there are the beginners and tourists who are craving information and eager to learn about how they can participate in a sport that has gained tremendous popularity in recent years. Now and then, you might even see a couple of kids drag a cooler full of menhaden through the door thinking their catch worthy of a spot on the shop photo board (so what?.... we had a great time catching them). There's no end to the revolving door and to the characters and personalities who pass through.

The proprietors are usually expert fishermen themselves, having through the years spent many hours in the surf fishing, trapping lobsters, and catching bait for the shop. There aren't many fishing techniques or procedures that they don't know and they know their island waters and the coastline like the backs of their hands. The shops' photo boards are an incredible look into the islands' fishing history and a testament to the possibilities awaiting an eager fisherman. Not that one would ever need incentive or encouragement to engage in this fine and challenging sport, but a few glances at the shop's photo board is usually enough to excite any angler.

The bait shops are also a significant source of island fishing history, especially when the proprietor has been in charge for many years. They have experienced firsthand what the fishing season brings each year — the fish, the weather, and the people. Some years are lean and some spectacular, but there are always many chapters in this tough, but adventurous lifestyle. I had the good fortune to know two such men on Jamestown and Block Island. They were fishing legends in their own right and their personalities, although different as night and day, added sparkle and charm to each island's community. Unfortunately, both have recently passed away; however, in 1987, by a stroke of luck, I filmed an interview on video with Rebelle Felice, the owner and proprietor of the bait shop in Jamestown during the '50s, '60s and '70s. He had retired from the bait shop by then and I was shooting segments for a fishing video that I was making as a Christmas gift. After watching the video again recently, I decided that his accounts of early island fishing were too valuable and precious not to pass along here.

Rebelle was born in Ancona, Italy, in 1911. He opened the Creek Bait Shop in Jamestown in May of 1954 with his wife, Leonora. As I mentioned earlier in the book, I first met Rebelle when I was about 17 years old and from the moment I met him, and to this day, I have never encountered anyone with a more vivacious personality — he was pure fire and brimstone — and his point of view was often accompanied with a barrage of colorful adjectives. His bait shop (where he also lived with his wife and three children) was not much more than a small wooden shack supported above the daily ebb and flow of the creek by pilings. The shop is still there today, located on the Great Creek off of North Main Road in Jamestown, and looking almost exactly as it did over 50 years ago.

Rebelle had discovered, along with one of his brothers, that the bass population around Jamestown during the 1950s was nothing short of spectacular. He turned fishing for bass into a second, and more profitable, business by fishing at night for stripers and running the bait shop during the day. While many of the wealthy residents and visitors to the island would fish from the bass stands erected by the island fishing clubs, Rebelle fished from a small boat at night. It was common for bass club members, with their personal assistants, to catch one or two fish on an outing; however, Rebelle was catching several hundred pounds of bass almost every night from several locations he had discovered around the island. The money from the sale of the fish helped him to sustain his family. He would also travel to the Cape Cod Canal to fish with his brother, where the bass were equally as plentiful. I asked him what might be an average night's success at the Cape Cod Canal and he said that he could almost always get all the small stripers that he wanted:

*"The fish were anywhere from 10 to 18 pounds. That's before anybody could reach the outer Cape. We'd catch bass for six hours. .....Yeah! Incoming full tide...... outgoing full tide. Right in the Cape Cod Canal!"*

What about in Jamestown?

*"There weren't that many people fishin'...... Me and my brother was one of the first ones to start fishin' bass* [It hadn't been a sport] *for the poor people. Before that it was a rich man's prize. They used to catch 'em off Beavertail. In other words, the* [assistants] *would chum the bass for them rich guys ....Arthur Clarke and all them people, ....they would chum, chum, chum, and they'd only get three or four bass, and that's it."*

Why wasn't everybody fishing for bass if there were so many of them?

*"People couldn't afford to. There was no rods, there was no reels ....it was just coming about then. That's why there was nobody fishin' for ' em. We used Cuttyhunk line that you used to have to wear a bib..... and a finger on the reel."*

And the bass were all over then?

*"....all over"*

Even in the Bay you could catch them?

*"Everywhere!! When we got the Creek* [Bait Shop] *in 1954, when we started fishin', they* [the bass] *were right in Sheffield [Cove]. I'd net for shiners and silversides at night and I'd get two or three bass in the net! You know, schoolies —— right on shore, right off of Mackerel Cove."*

What was your favorite bait when you used to fish for the big bass?

*"Plugs. A lot of eel skins on plugs."*

Did that work better than a popper?

*"....just an ordinary plug? Yeah. At night? Yeah, it was deadly. Right off the 'House on the Rocks' it was deadly, extremely deadly."*

Better than live eels?

*"We never used live eels. It was just strictly plugs with skins — at night."*

What was your best technique — how did you bring the plugs through the water?

*"Just cast it and reel in very slow. ....the plug did the rest because on accounta' that tail actin' as a rudder."*

A little tail of the eel skin, you mean?

*"Yeah, about that far from the plug....and it would sway beautiful. The plug would be that deep in the water and the bass would go crazy! Right off the 'House on the Rocks,' we'd get three or four hundred pounds of bass a tide!! Yes! And I taught these natives all the Goddammed tricks because they didn't know shit!"*

As I said, Rebelle was never afraid to tell you what was on his mind. But inside that crusty exterior was a man who would give you the shirt off his back. And he understood all too well that the striper resource was limited, as were the other species of fish that were sought after in the island's waters. Rebelle considered it his duty to watch over Jamestown's fishing resources and, even though it occasionally hurt his own pocket, he was always willing to be an advocate for whatever conservation measures were necessary to ensure a healthy fishery. He was truly a monarch of the island when it came to the fish and anyone who wanted to fish for them on *his* island.

When I interviewed Rebelle in 1987, the Atlantic Striped Bass Conservation Act, enacted by Congress, had already been in effect for three years. It forced coastal states to restrict or eliminate the commercial harvest and sale of striped bass and to impose restrictions and size limitations on recreational harvest of the fish as well. There was a lot of bait shop politicking going on over this subject because there were a lot of fishermen, both commercial and recreational, who couldn't understand the importance of time and restrictions necessary to allow the bass to make a comeback from near decimation. In 1987, the regulations in Rhode Island for striped bass were one fish per person per day and a 33-inch minimum. This was about the time that better numbers of smaller bass were starting to show up, probably due to a very good 1982 year class, but it was by no means a signal to open things back up — we still had a long way to go. A smattering of large bass had also been caught by surfcasters and reported in the spring of that year, making for a lot of bait shop chatter among fishermen about the necessity for the current restrictions. Well, Rebelle was one of the best when it came to bait shop politics and he *really did* know what he was talking about.

What about bluefish?

*"I hated the bastards! I don't fish for 'em now. They gotta realize one thing this year, the way they're fishin' the bluefish — they're gonna wipe them out too. Because fish is so high and so much in demand, they're already thinkin' they're gonna net 'em — they're gonna gill net 'em! Yes!"*

Somebody told me that they're trying to get the gill netters out of the Bay because they started netting tautog (blackfish) last year.

*"They started already. One guy in Newport.... four weeks ago, in just two weeks right off of Castle Hill.... he had a gill net there. He made $10,000 in two weeks!"*

On tautog?

*"Yes! A dollar a pound they're gettin'.... from 10 cents!"*

That'll wipe 'em out in no time at all.

*"Of course! Do they realize they had a survey about 21 years ago? Four thousand tautog/blackfish were tagged. Up there, up north, way up north and down south. And the farthest a tautog would travel was 20 miles away from home — that is it!"*

That's all their range is? Maybe from Providence to Brenton reef and that's it?

*"That's about it. And from the reef they'll go to Matunuck or they go to Block Island. And it takes a long time for a blackfish to reach 8 or 9 pounds. Very long time. They know all that! So what the hell are they having another survey for?*

Is that what they're doing? A survey to see whether or not they can net them?

*"They're taggin' 'em now. What the hell for? They did that. We did that. What are they gonna tag em again for? Waste another $15,000 or $20,000?*

*"Now they're taggin' flounder. Why the hell did they open the upper bay to let the draggers in to drag flounder?"*

What about the bass situation? At least things are starting to improve a little on that front.

*"But they want to open it."*

Do you think that there are enough people behind it to open it up?

*"Quite a few against it. Because it's like we said in the first place, it's fool's gold. It's the greed. They say now because they get a few 40 or 50 pounders, it's in the paper today, right there, look.... Just because they see a few 50-pounders, these Goddammed ignorant bastards, they want to bring it back to sell em! Yeah! They had a meetin' a couple of nights ago because some guys were gettin' ' em in their gill nets. They were fishing down by Sakonnet Point. You know what he recommended to do with em'? He was gettin' so many in the gill nets; he wanted to sell 'em for cat food!! I'm not kiddin' ya. So now they want to open it up — let's go hog wild!*

*"There's a lot of guys, like me, that are not fishin' for 'em on accounta that reason. Because we never used eels, we never used menhaden, we never used alewives. All we used was artificial lures — guys like Jerry Sylvester, Joe Tartorie and all* ***them*** *guys.* ***They*** *were bass fishermen! Not like these guys that goes out and gets a bucket full of menhaden and throws 'em at the bass — and the bass is stupid enough that it'll take anything alive. Them are not fishermen. That guy that got that 42-pounder the other day — he's not a fisherman. He got that with a herring! It's like giving you a cone of ice cream. Let that sonofabitch go out with a plug — and see what he does then!"*

Events on the island didn't always revolve around the fishing — just most of the time. But there were other things to deal with and sometimes these things took on a far greater importance than reeling in a fish. Severe storms pose a significant threat to communities that are surrounded by water and the pictures of what the hurricane of 1938 did to coastal Rhode Island are devastating illustrations of the kind of damage that can result. The 1938 storm (which took most by surprise) was a Category 3 hurricane with an eye that made a beeline right up the East Passage of Narragansett Bay and struck precisely at high tide. Another severe Category 3 hurricane (Hurricane Carol) hit the Bay in 1954 and it wreaked havoc along the coastline as well. The storm surge was an incredible 14 feet above the normal waterline.

How long ago was it when you started the bait shop?

*"May 1954. The year of the first hurricane we had. I was wiped out. In September the hurricane came — we got wiped out completely. I was fishin' Beavertail that morning. I had the Jeep and I got stuck in Mackerel Cove. Yeah! Right there!"*

The road washed out completely?

*"No. The Jeep stalled. I got out in the front and I put my rain gear cover over the hood and that heated the motor and dried it up — and I got across. And coming along in back of me* [was] *a lieutenant from the Radar Station. He got stuck, so he jumped out of the car. His car got washed into Scheffield's* [Cove] *and he got killed! And I just barely crossed.* [I] just *made it.*

*"We were fishing for bass. What made me quit was that we were casting 4-ounce jigs. We were casting, me and Manuel Tiexiera, he's dead now — we were casting jigs and the jigs wouldn't sink!! And the water was all brown. We were thinkin' what the hell is going on here?*

*"Stanley Popiel took Norman's boat around the other side and he rolled right around and he kept catchin' bass like you wouldn't believe! In that boat with Norman Olsen. Yeah! By the time I got to the bait shop.... some people had rescued my wife and three kids. When I got down there, there was a guy in a truck. A paneled truck. A Jewish fella from New York loaded with cigarettes — he was in the middle* [of the creek] *there. He couldn't come over. He couldn't cross — he would have drowned. So they put a rope around me and another guy — and I can't swim! And I tried to swim there. But we got dragged under, so they pulled the two of us in. Nobody had motorboats in them days to go get the guy, but finally they did get a line to him and pulled him ashore. They saved his life.*

*"So after the tide started going down we all met up at the fire barn. This Father Burns was there, he was.... well, he was an alcoholic. And this guy that we saved was there. He was gonna go back to New York and he was gonna sue the Town of Jamestown."*

What for?

*"He lost his cigarettes, he lost this and that. So we got around the fella.... the three or four of us.... Dr. Gobeille was there, and all of us, we told the guy, 'You sonofabitch, if you ever come back to Jamestown again, we'll kill you!' And the priest was right there! Drunk as a fart he was! .....because they were passin' liquor like mad, you know?!*

*" He never came back."*

That was the first year that you started the bait shop? Did you have to rebuild everything?

*"We lost everything. Worms were all over the place, money, dollar bills were floatin'. I stood on the steps and then sat down and they* [the rest of the family] *went to a home. But I wouldn't leave it."*

Do you miss it still?

*"Sure."*

You were there every day at 5 in the morning?

*"I slept there. We lived there! Me and my wife and three kids. Sometimes I'd get in from the House on the Rocks, I'd be fishin' all night and I'd get back at the shop just as the customers would start to come and be waitin' outside. And I'd have the Goddammed old truck full of bass. They were the days.*

*"It was a tough life, but it was a hell of a good one. You loved that life. I loved workin', and talking to people. I can't get on a pedestal in a hall and talk, but like, when you and I talk, I can do pretty good. Because I get all worked up, and sayin' bad words — that's right! If I feel like sayin' you're a prick, I'm gonna tell ya right to your face, and that's it! But that's the way it's got to be today. I'm sorry to tell you, but they don't wanna accept that."*

Rebelle passed away in November of 1999 at the age of 88. He was as much a part of Rhode Island history as the Newport mansions — where many of the elite had probably dined on his freshly caught bass! His passion and enthusiasm for life as a fisherman will be missed, but not forgotten.

**Rebelle Felice outside the Creek Bait**

**Rebelle inside the Creek Bait Shop with his wife, Leonora.**

Just as Jamestown had Rebelle, the Block has its monarchs of the island as well. Watching over the island's coastal waters, its fishermen, and the precious Great Salt Pond was the affable Matthew "Mac" Swienton and his son John. Mac and John owned and operated what was for many years the only bait shop on the island. It actually didn't start out as a bait and tackle shop; it started out 50 years ago as a sort of bed and breakfast named Twin Maples.

Mac was born in Taunton, Massachusetts, in December of 1916. After returning home from Army duty in World War II, Mac made frequent trips out to the Block for fishing and relaxation. That's where he met his wife, Madeleine. Madeleine was from one of the old-line Block Island families, the Cyrs. The Cyrs owned the Sea Breeze, which operated as a bed and breakfast in the 1940s; and Madeleine helped to run the business for the family. Shortly after Mac and Madeleine were married in the late 1940s, they purchased one of a series of buildings from the government that had been used by the Army as barracks during the war. They converted the building into a bed and breakfast and then over many years purchased and converted the remaining buildings on the property. Today, Twin Maples is a familiar Block Island landmark.

Once the bed and breakfast business became successful, Mac started the bait and tackle shop during the mid- to late-1950s with his son John. John remembers being involved with the bed and breakfast business and the bait shop from an early age. *"I grew up doing a lot of other people's dishes,"* he told me during a recent interview. He said, *"Back then, you could get a room for $45 a week and that included three meals a day! That lasted until the mid-1960s."*

I remember when I met Mac for the first time. I came into the bait shop expecting just about anything, based on my experiences with Rebelle. But Mac had a fatherly air about him. He was mild-mannered with sort of a distinguished-looking slant to his half-smile. He looked at me from behind the counter with genuine interest, but also with a suspicious eye that had probably become routine with him from having to deal with so many so-called " experts." When Mac learned that I was from Florida, we had a lot to talk about since fishing in Florida was something that he enjoyed very much. Unfortunately for Mac, he knew a lot more about fishing on the Block than I knew at that point about fishing the Florida grass flats.

Over the years, Mac became an expert at equipment repair. He could never understand how some fishermen could neglect the most essential pieces of their equipment that were ultimately necessary to ensure fishing success — the rod and reel. It got to the point where Mac would actually lecture his customers about the necessity of performing periodic maintenance on their equipment. He would often collect all the dirt and salt scale that he would remove from someone's reel and then save it in a little plastic bag, which he would give back to the customer along with a strong reprimand when he came in to pick up his reel. Some of the fishermen, fearing a scolding from Mac, would wait until the shop closed for the day and then drop off their reels in a bag on the front step of the shop with a note asking Mac to repair them. Most fishermen on the island knew that Mac had a knack for bringing crusty reels back from a state of severe misuse and they figured that it was better to take the tongue-lashing than to have to buy a new reel.

During the year's "in-season," there was a constant parade of fishermen, tourists, and other visitors coming into and out of the shop, and Mac's congenial personality and his penchant for conversation enabled him to accumulate a wide array of admiring friends. One such friend, and frequent visitor to the shop, was Brian Williams, NBC news anchor, who has visited the Block each summer for almost two decades. Knowing that Brian shared a special friendship with Mac, I caught up with him and asked him if he would be willing to reflect on his memories of Mac and the shop. I couldn't have agreed more with what he told me:

*"…. If you are a decent human with so much as half a heart and a brain in your head, how could you not admire that man from the first moment you entered that shop? To me, watching how people dealt with him was a test of character…, theirs, not his.*

*"I never knew him by any other name. Nor would I have ever dreamed of calling him anything other than 'Mr. Swienton.' I used to cringe when, while sitting off to the side in one of the beaten-up wooden chairs in his eclectic domain, I would watch people come in and treat this kind, dignified man as something somehow beneath them in the social pecking order. You could always tell when a major newspaper or magazine had just written a cover story on* [Block Island as] *'New England's Secret Gem' as the following week, or weekend, or summer would bring an influx of pasty-white Lower Manhattanites, sweating in black polo shirts, meticulously locking their bikes to the fence post, and striding into the fishing shack, determined to buy themselves a small piece of genuine New England. To my astonishment, his temperament never changed. He treated newcomers like regulars, and if you were in on the joke that was his dry sense of humor, all the better.*

*"If Twin Maples didn't exist, it would have to be invented. I always said that if Ralph Lauren had discovered it, fishing lures and faux fading photographs of lucky anglers would decorate every apartment on Manhattan's East Side. Twin Maples was always a kind of organized chaos. The cat that walked with a tremor. Sandy the golden retriever, whose mood was measurably brighter at the beginning of the tourist season, and who seemed to grow visibly tired of greeting admirers as August dragged on. The black surgical tubing that is still used to latch the fence to this day (just don't let Mac catch you forgetting to use it). The glass case, full of antique reels and lures…… and the t-shirts emblazoned with EAT FISH. You could even buy the same long-billed fishing hat that Mac wore. But try as you might to get it perfectly dirty and weather-beaten, it wouldn't make you any more like Mac.*

*"It was only after he died that I learned that Mac had seen horrifying action in the Pacific campaign during World War II. There is no way he would have told those stories while he lived. It didn't matter to him that my colleague, Tom Brokaw, had written a book that prompted WWII vets all over the country to finally open up and share those long-shut-away stories with loved ones; it wasn't what a quiet, taciturn, proud New Englander did. And Mac was all of those things.*

*"His hands looked like baseball mitts. You could almost make out fingers...... small protrusions on what were basically huge calluses. But what magic he could work with those gnarled hands. When presented with a tumbleweed of fishing line, tangled around the reel by a 6-year-old, and mixed with ice cream and fish scales, he would smile, grunt, and sit on his stool, knowing full well it would take pliers, a magnifying glass, and the better part of an hour to untangle. For his efforts, and the tackle that was lost when 'the big one got away,' he would charge all of $1.25. I don't think he ever asked for a larger amount. Over the years, he gave away tons of free bait, fixed thousands of snarled lines, and taught countless thousands of first-timers how to at least TRY to catch a fish.*

*"Twin Maples was his domain, and Mac was its CEO. In that respect, it perfectly reflected the boss — plain, uncomplicated, weather-beaten, and utilitarian. And just like the boss, it was built to last. It never called attention to itself, but on a sunny summer afternoon at high tide, it's hard to imagine a better place on earth. Or a better man."*

To be sure, Mac kept his finger on the pulse of the island's fishing resources and a watchful eye on the Great Salt Pond, which was his backyard for the greater part of his life. If you were doing something in or to the pond that you shouldn't have been doing, or conducting your activities in any manner that was disrespectful or damaging to the island, you would sooner or later have to answer to Mac — and if you thought your hide would be tanned for a dirty reel, you were in for the monarch's wrath if you hurt his backyard. Mac died in April of 2000; he was 83. His interests were not only fishing, but the community as well, and he gave his time to the community as a volunteer fireman and a fan of the school's team sports. As remarkable as it may be, the only time Mac ventured off the island during the last five years of his life was to watch the school's basketball team compete for the state championship. They won.

**John and Mac Swienton in front of Twin Maples Bait and Tackle Shop.**

Mac's son, John, took over the daily management and operation of Twin Maples many years prior to his father's death. I spoke with John not long ago about the early years of running the shop. One of the first things he told me was that unlike the way visitors to the island see it in the summer, the rest of the year was difficult — especially during the early, formative years of Twin Maples.

*"It was tough to make any money; we had to do everything we could to economize. I would go out and dig clams to sell for bait and we'd use the empty soda cans that we sold in the shop as containers to put 'em in. I would also get squid from the draggers down in the harbor to sell for bait. In the wintertime, there was basically no income, so what you made in the summer had to hold you through until the next year."*

When he was just a young kid, John started lobstering from a small skiff. As he grew older, he developed his lobster trapping into a four-boat commercial business. However, when Mac had to have triple bypass surgery, John had to spend more time operating the rental cottages and the bait shop, so the lobster business went by the wayside. The lobster business was tough work, but it was lucrative. Even so, John felt that the lobster business was becoming very difficult. With each passing year, more and more time was required, but with the end result being fewer and fewer of the crustaceans in the traps.

*"At first, around the island, it was only the locals that were gettin' lobsters. They would put the traps in, say, April 1 and they would start producing and selling in about two weeks. The traps would be pulled for winter and then the cod fishing would begin. For some of the island guys, fishin' and lobsterin' was the only way to make ends meet. I had a guy that would come with me for two days a week to lobster from 5 in the morning to 1 in the afternoon. Then he would go to the airport to work until 5, and then fish for three hours to get bass to sell.*

*"When faster boats and better equipment came about, it hurt us because guys from the mainland that had this stuff found out that the Block Islanders weren't trapping lobster year 'round. They came over here and trapped all winter and that really hurt the numbers.*

*"Another thing that had a major effect* [on the industry] *were metal traps. Before that, traps were all made of wood. One major storm, and many would be destroyed. It would take a long time to build back the supply, so when that happened, it sort of evened out the pressure on the lobsters. Wire traps last a good long time, but two seasons is about all you can get out of a wooden trap."*

As many casual observers have noticed, the number of lobster pots in Rhode Island and New England waters today is staggering. I used to think there were a lot 10 years ago, but today there are so many traps that I can't believe the lobster population will be able to survive much longer at this pace. I made the comment to John that at least it must have been nice for him and his family to have all those wonderful lobster dinners.

*"I've never had a lobster. Really. I never had a hot, cooked lobster in my life. Well, maybe a few times, but that was when it was really cold and in a salad and with mayonnaise and stuff. Our family had lobsters at the dock all the time — we would never think of eatin' 'em."*

Imagine that?!

The Twin Maples clientele was — and still is — as diverse as it is loyal. Only a small proportion comes from Rhode Island, with the majority coming from New Jersey, New York, Connecticut, and more recently from New Hampshire, Vermont and Maine. John explained that the reason most of his guests visited the island was for the fishing — the lore of the Block's good striper fishing was well known to fishermen even back in the '50s. In fact, he told me that even before Twin Maples opened, many fishermen in the '30s and '40s already knew about the island's great fishing and were coming out on a regular basis to stay and fish. The regulars at Twin Maples were serious about the fishing and they would fish almost every night during their stay.

*"The guys would all bring their own outboard motors and rent the boats from me and my father. Every morning they would all get in their boats and either fish the* [Great Salt] *Pond or off the town dump. At night it was Sandy Point* [not in their boats, but on foot]. *They all went out there — it was always Sandy Point at night. The men would go to Black Rock during the day with their families, but for serious fishin', it was always Sandy Point."*

One of John's loyal customers was the late Ben Lubell. Ben would come out to the Block every year and stay at Twin Maples for the entire summer, along with many of his friends.

*"Ben fished seven days a week, and all day long for the 26 summers that he stayed with us. He kept accurate records in a log book. He wrote everything down. Time, temperature, the weather, and what he caught. One of his rules of thumb was when a bright moon was out he always used a blue-and-white popper. If it was dark with no moon, switch to a swimmer.*

*"He was one of those guys who could walk into a line of other fishermen and be the first one to catch fish, and he would catch the most. I asked him about that once and he said that he thought that one of the reasons might be because he was able to get just a little more distance* [on his casts] *than the others because he used 12-pound test* [line] *instead of 15- or 20-pound like the other guys. I was talkin' to Ben one day and I told him that I was out of bait for my lobster traps — I had about 400 of 'em too. Ben asked me if bluefish would work and I said sure. In just two days that man came in here with 200 bluefish!*

*"Ben had a system. He always used a popper and he never used to take the plugs out of the bluefish while they were alive. He told me that you waste too much time trying to do that. He would bring in a box of bluefish and they would all have plugs stuck in their mouths! Ben had a box of poppers that he kept in the boat or his truck and they were all lined up in rows of individual sleeves."*

In addition to advice and information regarding the whereabouts of the fish, many fishermen rely on the recommendations of the bait shop proprietor for tackle, especially in reference to plug selection. It has been said often that different plugs, and different colors, work better in different environments. Not that I ever believed in that theory, but there are enough fishermen that subscribed to those beliefs that John had to carry a selection of plugs to fit the fishermen's fancy for color and seasonality.

*"They say dark nights — dark plugs, bright nights light plugs. Here's how the system works for what I order and what seems to sell; you go black to*

*light to black. Black in the spring and fall, and light or bright in between. Back in the '50s and '60s, the guys that came out here hardly ever used bait. They used surface plugs like the Polaris or the Danny for example. In the summer, it was mostly 2-ounce poppers. The islanders on the other hand would use a variety of different baits — one of the more popular was eel skins pulled over Atom swimmers. The guys from Long Island were different — they liked yellow and pink needlefish."*

I asked John what he thought the most popular plug was today as opposed to many years ago.

*"They are the same — the same plug. The 2-ounce Atom popper.*

*"If I had a choice, and you said* [to me] *you're never gonna see another tackle shop, so what lures would you take with you, I would grab a bunch of Hopkins metal, a bunch of 2-ounce Atom poppers and the Atom swimmers — you know, the blue-and-white ones."*

Although some things never seem to change, there is no question that the striper fishing today is different than the striper fishing of many years ago. Today there are many more small stripers around the islands than there were 30 years ago, which is a very good thing, and fishermen nowadays are fishing more for the sport (and an occasional dinner fish), and not for the money the bass used to bring in the commercial markets. John agreed, saying that when he was growing up, small stripers were not very common on the Block.

*"We hardly ever saw small fish taken out here. It wasn't until the mid-'80s that smaller bass were more common — you know, schoolies. A small bass until then would have been a 25-pounder. We'd feel guilty about takin' a 25- or 30-pound bass because there were so many 40- and 50-pound fish around. We weighed in at least one 50-pounder a week — and that was all season, sometimes several a week — especially in the fall and early spring. The big ones would come in around the second and third week in June and the biggest bass of the year between Thanksgiving and mid-December.*

*"At one point, these guys were gettin' over $2 a pound for a whole fish. With five or six fish between 30 and 50 pounds, it doesn't take much to figure that in one good night they could have made some nice money — which they did often. There were sometimes bad feelings between some of the islanders and the off-island fisherman cause of what some of 'em* [the off-Islanders] *did. They would try to follow the island guys around to see where they were catchin' their fish — they'd even wait for 'em to leave the bait shop so they could follow 'em. The island guys had some tricks, though — some of them painted their trucks flat black to make it difficult to see where they were going or where they were parked. Or sometimes they would get dropped off*

*and picked up from a spot so others that drove by would think that no one was there fishing."*

I asked John if there was any significant catch or blitz that stood out in his mind from the past 30 years or so. He said that no one catch came right to mind — there were so many of them that they all seemed to run together. One he did eventually mention was a night many years ago when his cousin and a couple of other guys caught over 50 stripers in one night with none being less than 40 pounds! Is it any wonder that John or Mac have never fished anywhere else in Rhode Island (or in New England for that matter)? And also interesting is the fact that neither Mac nor John had ever met or knew of Rebelle. Wouldn't that have been some interesting conversation?!

**The bait and tackle shop trophy photo board at Twin Maples.**

# Chapter VII

## The Blitz

One of the most spectacular fishing events that nature provides those who are lucky enough to be in the right place at the right time is the incredible fishing bonanza often referred to as "the blitz." No matter how experienced a fisherman you are, there is no way to predict a blitz. You can never tell when or where a blitz will happen or how long it will last. But one thing about a blitz is always a certainty — anyone who's fortunate enough to have had the experience will remember it for the rest of his life.

For the surfcaster, a blitz is best defined as an event when the Fishing Gods get together and smile on a small section of the coastline. The resulting effect is that no matter how many guys are there, the fish outnumber the fishermen exponentially. The fish are voraciously hungry, they strike at anything you throw at them, and you're onto a fish with almost every cast. Most blitzes occur because a large school of stripers or bluefish, or both, has pinned a school of baitfish against a stretch of shoreline; the larger fish hammer away at the baitfish until they're gone, or until they somehow manage to escape to return once again to open water. A blitz can also be an event where the fish, for some reason, remain in one area in an unusually high concentration for an extended period of time — sometimes for more than a month, as Frank Daignault and others discovered in Provincetown out on the Cape in 1977, one of the biggest and longest striped bass blitzes in history. The true blitz, however, is usually short-lived and the fish are fast and furious in their feeding action. And whereas darkness is usually a requirement for great striper fishing, a blitz can happen at any time, day or night. One of the more interesting and exciting characteristics of the true blitz is that the predator fish, usually bass or blues, seem to lose all sense of caution and will viciously attack anything that remotely resembles the baitfish they're chasing, sometimes for hours on end. The phenomenon very much resembles that of a school of piranha attacking prey in the Amazon. Bluefish, in fact, will continue to feed on baitfish even after they become completely full, to the point that ingested baitfish will actually be spilling from their gill slots because there's no more space in their gullets or stomachs. On many occasions, I have pulled blitzing bluefish up onto the beach as they spewed bait from almost every opening on their bodies. They are amazing creatures.

Sometimes a blitz comes about when only a small number of fish have cornered a bait school in a small cove or other quasi-contained area of shoreline. Such was the case one afternoon when I was fishing Block Island's south shore with Max Fahnestock, a former client, and now close friend. It was late October and Max and I had decided to go over to the Block ahead of the rest of the guys to get things set up in the house we had rented. We must have finished the chores early because we ended up at Black Rock that afternoon. I remember that when we arrived at the water, several guys from another group were already fishing just below the base of the parking area. They were bait-fishing with mackerel chunks, but they hadn't caught any fish yet, so we headed east down the beach to an empty cove. Once we rounded the corner into the cove, we lost sight of the other guys and we couldn't tell if they were picking up any fish or not. During the first half-hour of fishing, neither Max nor I had a single hit, but the conditions looked promising. It was an hour before high tide and the surf was becoming very active from the effects of an approaching front. Sure enough, just as if the Fishing Gods had flipped the switch, the fish arrived with surprising suddenness. It wasn't a full-out blitz, but on about every fourth or fifth cast one of us had a fish on, and although the bass we were catching weren't cows, they were nice fish (between 15 and 20 pounds). I also noticed that, as the afternoon progressed, the fish seemed to be increasing in size. Max had already decided to keep two fish (we needed to stock up on a few fillets for the crew coming over that evening) and I had a nice 20-pounder up on the rocks, but something told me not to take the other of my two-fish limit, at least not just yet. The fishing continued that afternoon at a healthy pace for almost a solid hour. The bass had come into this cove, they had found something they liked, and they had decided to stay. Just about at the top of the tide, I had a nice hit at the end of my cast — almost immediately after my lure hit the water. When I set the hook, the big bass was so surprised that it lunged halfway out of the water, creating a terrific splash just before bolting for the depths.

It was an exhilarating fight — my heart always races when I've got a big fish on. It's so much more of a challenge to land a big fish when you're fishing with a plug because you never really know where in the fish those hooks have set. Usually when you get the fish to shore, the plug won't be swallowed or totally within its mouth; most of the time, it will be partially *outside* its mouth. And at least 90% of the time, the fish will have hit the head of the plug and, as a consequence, will be hooked with the front treble. It's a natural (perhaps innate) behavior of many game fish to do this. And unlike fishing with bait, the striper doesn't have enough time to swallow a lure before you set the hooks — at least if you do it correctly — and while that may reduce the mortality of the fish that are released, it gives the fish a greater opportunity to get rid of those hooks on the way in or, as some big fish do, on the way out. Before I started to change the hooks on all of my lures to Owner 4X-strong trebles, I would show people the hooks that bass had straightened and they would laugh and say, "There's no way a fish could do that." But believe me, the bass do it. Big stripers are so strong, and their jaw structure is so tough, that they instinctively try to snag the trailing hooks of any lure attached to the side of their face on the nearest rock or seaweed bed and, when successful, they don't seem to have any problem ripping the lure from their mouth and straightening several of the hooks in the process.

On this day, the bass didn't have luck on her side and she was beached after an admirable battle that thoroughly exhausted one excited surf fisherman. When I first saw the fish, I was hoping that it might weigh in at around 40 pounds, and indeed it did — an even 42 pounds. The interesting thing was that our little mini-blitz was very cove-specific. I was thinking that the guys we saw when we first arrived at Black Rock that afternoon must have hammered the bass with their baits, but it wasn't so. When Max and I rounded the corner on our way back to the truck, the other guys hadn't had a single hit. When they saw the four beautiful stripers we were carrying back to the truck, their mouths dropped open in disbelief. But don't ever believe that there isn't an element of luck associated with fishing — it could just as easily have happened the other way around. As it is so often said, that's why the sport is called "fishing" and not "catching."

**The author with a nice 42-pounder caught during a mini-blitz at Black Rock one October afternoon.**

Over the past 30 years, there have been some spectacular blitzes that are now part of surf fishing history. The famous blitzes are remembered because of the enormous size of some of the fish that were caught as well as because of the sheer number of fish that were landed. One such blitz is the famous Columbus Day blitz of 1981. It happened on the south shore of Martha's Vineyard and, like so many other blitzes, there were no signs that foretold what was about to happen on that day. The blitz occurred on the south shore of the Vineyard between Homer's Pond and Tisbury Great Pond. Apparently a few bass in the 40-pound range were taken the evening before by a couple of guys who were fishing there during the night, but the big blitz didn't start until just after sunrise on Columbus Day. Those who were present (and unfortunately, I wasn't) all say the same thing: "It all just started to happen." That morning, there were only a few "regulars" fishing the beach. Eventually, they all spotted a large school of menhaden that was being attacked by a much larger school of striped bass. The first few bass were taken by one of the guys who was snagging the menhaden with a weighted treble hook and then casting the snagged baitfish back to the hungry stripers. As the pod of baitfish moved in and out along the shoreline, the fisherman started to hammer away at the bass, discovering that most of the stripers were 30- and 40-pounders! Shortly after that, another school of menhaden appeared farther down the beach and these, too, were being attacked by the huge marauding stripers.

Well, I don't know how this always seems to happen, but as soon as the fish arrive in big numbers, an otherwise isolated stretch of beach with relatively few fishermen becomes a fishermen's convention. And that was the case on this day, but of course, who would blame anyone for wanting to participate in what would eventually go down as one of the biggest bass blitzes in history? In this instance, some of the guys who had been fishing there when the blitz began had to leave to go to work. When they arrived back in town and spread the word, anyone who could drop what he was doing did so and headed for the beach. In fact, folks flying onto the island later that day said how unusual it was to see more than 30 beach buggies out on the beach in the middle of a bright and sunny day. The blitz lasted until well into the late afternoon with only brief lulls. And the next day, the fish were gone, just as suddenly as they had arrived.

The accounts of the number of fish taken on that day vary depending upon which fisherman you talk to (imagine that?). Some of the guys had 15 to 20 huge bass each. There were at least six or seven stripers taken that were over 50 pounds, and between 200 and 300 bass that were over 30 pounds, with a good portion of those over 40! Of course, in those days, there were no limits and to make ends meet, a lot of the fishermen relied upon the extra income derived from selling the bass they caught. Today, I'm quite certain that those fishermen who were present at the Columbus Day blitz would not be proud of the damage done to the resource. On *that* day, however, it would have been easy to have gotten caught up in the excitement of such an incredible blitz. I'm sure that I would've been right there with them, catching as many as I could and looking for the *really* big one in the school.

A little less than two weeks following the Columbus Day blitz, another blitz of huge stripers occurred on the Cape at Nauset Beach. This blitz may very well have been the granddaddy of them all as far as numbers of large bass are concerned. While the Columbus Day blitz had less than a dozen fish landed that were over fifty pounds, the Nauset Beach blitz yielded close to 70 fish that weighed more than 50 pounds, several that were *60* pounds, and several hundred bass that were 30- and 40-pounders! Even more remarkable is the fact that this blitz was on and off for over a week!

My first encounter with blitzing stripers was certainly nothing like that. However, no matter where you are, or how large or small the fish may be, when you first realize that you have encountered a big group of fish "on the feed," the excitement is overwhelming. Very early in my years of fishing the Rhode Island coastlines, while I was attending the University of Rhode Island, I had the good fortune to find a small house for rent on the southernmost end of Point Judith. The house was right on the ocean, positioned on a bluff about 30 feet above the water. There was a large picture window in the living room through which you could look out over a beautiful and wide expanse of the sea. I did a lot of my studying in the living room because of the abundance of light the window let in. One warm and sunny September afternoon, I looked up from my work and stared out of the picture window over the ocean. The surf was relatively calm with small breakers slowly cascading into sheets of whitewater as they reached for shore. Suddenly, about 100 yards out from the surf line, I could see something that was sporadically breaking the smooth contour of the waves. They were fish, and lots of them, smacking the water's surface as they chased bait. I didn't notice them at first because the feeding action was inconsistent, on and off every minute or so, and I was thinking that because it was daytime, this was probably a school of bluefish. So I jumped up to go get my fishing rod, which was always kept nearby and rigged with a blue-and-white Atom popper. I flew out the door and down the pathway on the side of the bluff only to realize that when I had arrived at the water's edge, the fish had moved farther offshore and about 50 yards beyond my casting range. How frustrating! There they were, right out in front of me, taunting me with their sudden strikes at the baitfish. Finally, I just couldn't stand it any longer. I decided that since the contour of the bottom sloped gradually away from the house, I would bite the bullet and try to wade out to within casting distance of these fish. I managed to get about 20 yards out in waist-deep water just before the first larger-than-expected breaker greeted me in the chest. But it didn't matter; it didn't faze me with all the adrenaline that was going through my body at that moment. And as luck would have it, while I was wading out, the fish moved in closer and I was now within casting range. As I started to cast to the feeding fish, I got a sudden glimpse of several fish in the roll of an incoming wave — they were not bluefish, they were stripers! But what appeared to be impending success was far from it. The bass didn't want anything to do with the popper. After four or five casts into and around the school, my heart began to sink — I couldn't get the fish to strike. Finally, after more than a dozen casts, and as the school began to once again move farther from shore, I had a strike, and then a fish on. It was at that point that I remembered that I was still standing in waist-deep water and had no way to control this fish if, and when, I managed to get it close to me. Of course, the smartest thing would have been to gradually back into shore and then beach the fish. But I was too excited to think about that, and when I got the fish to within a few feet of me, I tucked my rod under one arm and reached down and grabbed the bass with both arms in a tight bear hug, after which I started a rapid trek back to shore. This was not very smart considering that the fish still had a plug with two treble hooks hanging out of its mouth. Luckily, there was no one around to witness this amateurish and comical display; however, if anyone had been watching, he would've had a good chuckle. Nonetheless, as the blitzing stripers moved completely out of casting range, I made it back to shore with what turned out to be a very, very special 22-pound striped bass — and one most deserving of a bear hug. No matter how big, or how small, you never forget your first keeper bass. It was indeed a fine September afternoon.

I have experienced many more bluefish blitzes than striped bass blitzes. That's probably because a lot of my surf fishing was done during the years when the bluefish population had made a tremendous comeback from the dismal '60s and early '70s, when it was relatively uncommon to catch one.

In fact, one of the largest blitzes that I've ever seen involved a massive bluefish blitz that occurred along the Narragansett Town Beach. It was mid-October 1984, and I had invited one of my very best friends and fishing partners from Tampa, Richard Michalski, to join me for a long weekend of fishing on Jamestown Island. Richard and I met playing tennis when I first moved to Tampa many years ago, and I learned shortly after meeting him that he was an avid fisherman who loved to fish the mangrove flats along Florida's Gulf coast. Since he shared all of his Florida techniques and fishing spots with me, I thought it was only appropriate that I invite him to visit Jamestown for what I told him, in jest, was "real men's fishing." I used to tease him, often telling him that the small speckled trout, redfish and snook that we caught along the Gulf coast of Florida could be used for striper bait in New England. Curiosity got the better of him and he finally agreed to come and see what this striper fishing was all about. Well, aside from the fact that Richard had never fished with an 11-foot surf rod, didn't really like the cold, and couldn't imagine that a fish could see — let alone strike — a lure in heavy surf in the middle of the night; he was otherwise perfectly receptive to these new methods and techniques. We were staying at the Shepleys' house on Jamestown from which, I told him, we would leave at around 4:30 the next morning to try our luck at the Point Judith lighthouse. When he asked why so early, I explained that "first light" in the fall had been a particularly productive time for me in the past, and besides, it would be Saturday morning, and we would want to try to beat the crowd there. He looked at me to see whether I was kidding and said, "The crowd, huh? Ok, if you say so."

We arrived at the Point Judith light the next morning at about 5:30 a.m. It was dark, it was raining, it was about 48 degrees, and there was no one in the parking lot next to the Coast Guard station. I told Richard that we should go ahead and put our chest waders on and get down to the shoreline before the others arrived. He glanced over at me with a half-smile and said, "There's nobody coming out here in the middle of the night — let's at least wait until there's a little daylight." No sooner had the words left his mouth than did three cars full of fishermen pull up into the parking lot, one after the other. And anyone could see from their swift and deliberate actions that these guys were in a hurry to get down to the water. Richard and I managed to reach the surf just ahead of everyone else; however, it was still pitch-black and I could see that he had no confidence that we were doing anything but wasting our time. I told him not to worry that it was dark, and to cast his Atom swimmer straight out in front of where he was standing, and then to bring it back in with a slow retrieve. As miracles go, he had hooked a bluefish on his very first cast. As he pulled the 10-pounder up onto the beach, the look of satisfied astonishment was all I could see. A miracle it was, too, because in the next two hours of fishing that morning, no one caught another fish.

So the tone of the morning was set — an awful lot of work for one miserable bluefish. After two hours, we left the surf at the lighthouse to go back to the car, along with several other guys who had arrived along with us that morning, and who were also now somewhat discouraged — their walking pace considerably slower than when they arrived. On the way back, I drove the scenic coastal route to Jamestown since Richard had never visited New England. About halfway back, we decided to stop at a favorite breakfast spot that was close to the Narragansett Town Beach — we never made it there. As we rounded the bend just beyond the Coast Guard Restaurant, we saw a scattered group of about 20 fishermen on the rocks behind the seawall, with rods flying in all directions, many rods with serious bends. From the looks of things, a few guys must have discovered the blitzing fish and then, as more and more fishermen drove by, they just pulled their cars right up on the sidewalk, jumped the seawall, and started casting — which is exactly what we did. We didn't know it right away, but this was an enormous school of very large bluefish and the blues had a very large school of menhaden pinned against the rocks, stretching all along the seawall and far down the length of Narragansett Town Beach. Richard and I each hooked onto a fish right away, but I started to realize that since we were standing on slippery rocks just below the seawall, it was going to be difficult to land a fish and then have to deal with these thrashing and snapping alligator-blues from the rocks. So I motioned to Richard to follow me down onto the beach where we would try our luck from a more stable vantage point. It didn't make any difference; the fishing was great from the beach as well. There was a blue waiting to strike on every cast, no matter where you stood, and dragging them up on the sand was far easier than trying to do a balancing act on the slime-covered rocks. The bluefish were so thick and so aggressive that they were driving the menhaden into the shallow surf line and causing them to jump out of the water and onto the sand. I remember looking over at the rocks around the seawall, where even more fishermen had now gathered. Everyone who drove by and happened to have a rod with him was getting into this. There were kids, guys in office clothes, mothers, even a guy in a suit who had taken off his coat and rolled up his pants in order to get out there and cast (there was a picture of him in the *Providence Journal* the next day). Beached ("sidewalked") bluefish were everywhere — hundreds of them. Richard had never seen anything like this in his life, and neither had I — not of this magnitude.

In less than an hour, we both had a nice pile of very large bluefish on the beach behind us and we were starting to get tired of pulling these alligators in. My lures were in shambles; I don't think that I had any left that didn't have bent or broken-off hooks. Richard was getting so tired that he started to hook his fish, and instead of reeling it in, he was turning around, putting the rod on his shoulder, and walking up the beach in order to drag the fish ashore. Seeing this, I knew it was time to stop. It was no longer a sport at this point; it was too easy. We had each caught about 20 bluefish, which were all going back to the house to be filleted. It felt as if it took forever and a day to drag the fish, four at a time, back to the truck. Mary Shepley was going to be elated with all this fresh fish. Not one would be wasted as long as she had anything to say about it.

**This was the scene for about a quarter of a mile along the Narragansett Beach seawall on the day of the great bluefish blitz. It's hard to see them, but there are piles of bluefish scattered throughout the rocks. Notice the guy in the coat and tie at the picture bottom — he just had to stop and fish!**

Just before we left the seawall in Narragansett that morning, I noticed a little boy about 8 years old, standing with his mother on the sidewalk next to our truck. He had what appeared to be a small freshwater Zebco rod-and-reel outfit, the kind with the thumb depressor on the back of the reel. He was crying because he didn't have a lure to use. Seeing this, I reached into the back of the truck and grabbed a small Atom swimmer that had been cracked at the midsection and thoroughly mangled by one of the big chopper bluefish. The lure still had a wire leader attached to it, but that really wasn't going to matter considering the very old 8-pound test line that was threaded on the boy's reel.

I rigged the mangled swimmer to the boy's rod and told him that I was going to cast the lure out for him and then hand him the rod, explaining that although he might not land the fish he hooked, he would certainly have a thrill from feeling the power that these big blues have. Sure enough, as soon as the lure hit the water, a bluefish inhaled it, and was off and running. I quickly handed the rod back to the boy and told him to hold on tight, and if the bluefish stopped running, then he could try and reel — of course, it didn't. To this day, I have never again seen water vapor and other stuff shoot out from a reel like that! It took the bluefish all of about five seconds to literally smoke every bit of line from that reel (which needed new line anyway) and then with a sudden forward jerk and a solid *poink*, the line snapped and the fish was gone, only to leave one 8-year old with a memory he'll never forget.

**Richard Michalski and the author displaying about half of the bluefish bounty from the incredible blitz earlier that day.**

When Richard and I left Narragansett Town Beach that morning, the blitz was still in progress. I don't know how many more hours it lasted, but I knew that we certainly had all the fishing action we could handle for one morning. When we arrived back at the Shepleys' house, Bill greeted us with fillet boards and sharpened knifes and we all went to work on the fish. There was one fish, however, that I pulled out of the bunch because it was larger than any of the others — definitely the biggest bluefish that I had ever caught. I asked Bill to get out a fish scale so that we could determine its weight and he produced the only one he had, which measured up to a 30-pound capacity. We attached the scale to a sturdy nail protruding from one of the basement beams and then hoisted this big blue up to see what it weighed. When the scale bottomed out at 30 pounds, we couldn't believe our eyes! It looked as if we had a new state record, and maybe even a new world record for rod and reel! The basement crew became electrified with excitement as we tried to figure out how we could get this fish to a certified scale. Then Bill remembered that even though Rebelle had closed the island's bait shop for the season, he had taken the scale, which was still certified, back to his house, which was only a few blocks away. When Bill explained the situation to Rebelle over the phone, he told Bill to bring the bluefish right over. By the time we made it over to Rebelle's house, Rebelle had phoned a few of his friends who he knew would be interested in seeing a world-record fish. We pulled up in front of Rebelle's house and the garage door was open where he and several of his friends were now waiting inside the garage with a ready scale. I took the blue out of the truck and started walking down the driveway with it. As I got about halfway to the house, from inside the garage I heard Rebelle bark out in his usual gruff voice, "Where's the Goddamn 30-pounder?" And I replied, "Well, here, this is it." And as the words left my mouth, I could see Rebelle's friends shaking their heads down at the floor with sarcastic smiles. Rebelle grabbed the fish in disgust and said, "This ain't no Goddamn 30-pound fish! What the hell's the matter with you guys?" Rebelle was, of course, quite correct — he had seen enough 30-pound fish in his day to know what one looked like. In fact, this bluefish weighed just a hair shy of 20 pounds on *his* scale.

When we returned to Bill's house, embarrassed and downtrodden, we discovered that Bill's scale was so old and rusted from being in the basement that the internal spring had broken under the weight of the bluefish, causing the scale to permanently bottom out at 30 pounds. We can all laugh about it now, but since then, I assure you that there's been a new, first-class, well-maintained fish scale at the house — ready for the next world record.

Just as it is fortunate and exhilarating to have been involved in a blitz, it is almost unthinkable to know that you missed one by a week, or a day, or, as I once did, by being on the wrong side of the island. It was during the first week of November in 1986. I had made the trip out to Block Island one or two days before Halloween, and the day after I arrived, a nor'easter blew in and stopped the ferry from running for several days. The fishing was slow with the heavy winds from the storm; however, after things settled down, I had heard from some of the other fishermen that the guys who were fishing Southwest Point the previous night did quite well. I found out later that word of their success had spread all over the island and lots of guys were planning to fish the Point the next night. Since I don't like to fish in a crowd or in a line, I elected to fish elsewhere that evening and I missed what was later described as an incredible blitz of huge bass in historic numbers. Harvey happened to be out at his house on the Point that evening and he told me later that there were at least 20 cars and trucks parked down below his house and as many as 40 guys lined up all around the Point fishing. He said that he remembers when he went down to the water with his two sons to see what was going on, he had to step over the stripers that were scattered all over the shore, some of which were bigger than his kids. I shudder to think of fishing shoulder to shoulder like that, in a huge line of guys, some knowing what they're doing and some not. And I can't imagine what it must have been like with all those big fish on, several at a time, with crossed lines and, most likely, crossed tempers. Nevertheless, missing out on the opportunity to hook into big bass is never a pleasant thought — especially when they are practically right under your nose.

I've saved my best blitz story for last, and it's the best for several reasons. First, because I had the privilege of sharing it with my two best friends; second, because it removed a stigma from one fisherman that had been carried around for over twenty years, and third, because in the end, only three fish were kept. It happened out on Block Island during the fourth week of October in 1993, when Raymond, Bruce, and I were staying at Harvey's place for the week. The three of us had taken the ferry over to the Block ahead of Bruce's father and uncle, who were to join us on the island the next day. We decided to unpack that afternoon and get settled into the house, have a nice dinner, and then do a little fishing down on the Point in front of the house. However, there wasn't much action that evening at Southwest Point. I think Bruce caught a couple of small bass, but that was about it, so we all decided to call it a night and planned to leave for other spots around the island early the next morning. The next day brought a crisp 20-knot northeast wind with it and for some reason, as our first stop, we chose to fish in the teeth of it out at Sandy Point. It was about 4:30 a.m. when we arrived just beyond the North Light and still completely dark. I don't know what the wind-chill factor is at 46 degrees with a 20-knot wind, but it felt bitterly cold and miserably uncomfortable. My attention was temporarily diverted from the conditions by a sudden strike that came from the whitewater of the rip where I had cast. It was a nice bluefish, about 10 pounds, and I was hoping that it was an omen of things to come. I dragged the fish back up to the truck and, when I turned around to go back out to the rip, I could see Raymond's faint outline against the horizon, standing, rod bent forward, with a fish on — which, considering his record, was in itself a very good omen. He was onto another bluefish, which turned out to be about the same size as mine. Things were certainly beginning to look promising — until we fished for the next half-hour with no further success. And by this time, the wind was beginning to chip away at our stamina, so when one of the guys suggested that we leave in search of more comfortable fishing conditions, he received no resistance. We decided to go to Black Rock because we suspected that the contour of the island bluffs might give us a little relief from the wind. When we arrived at the Black Rock parking area, it was still dark, and we were pleased to see that there was only one other truck there. We got our gear together, climbed down the cliff, and headed off to one of the coves we liked to fish. As it turned out, even though the high bluffs did offer some protection against the wind that morning, I remember that it was still quite windy and the surf was very active with white water everywhere. When we reached the cove, Bruce and Raymond decided to have a cigarette and wait for a little daylight before climbing out on the rocks to cast. I will never forget the three of us, nonchalantly leaning against the bluff wall that morning, and with no urgency whatsoever to get our lines into the water — if we had only known what was out there waiting for us! We never imagined that the rocky surf in front of us was teeming with 30- and 40-pound striped bass, already involved in a major blitz.

Finally, Raymond meandered down to one end of the cove and perched himself atop a large rock at the base of the breaking surf while Bruce and I continued to chat. Then, Bruce and I, realizing that daylight was upon us at this point, selected casting rocks and started going at it. But no sooner had I released my first cast, than I heard a sharp whistle pierce the morning air. It was Bruce, motioning to me to look beyond him and down into the cove. There, with his knees bent, leaning back for leverage, was Raymond with a huge bow in his rod and a serious fish on the line. After more than 20 years of the worst fishing luck I have ever known a man to have, it was a fine sight to behold. However, within seconds, Bruce and I were both hit and were likewise onto nice fish, so our attention was quickly diverted to the more pressing matters at hand. It was a sight that I will never forget — the three of us, with bent rods, grinning ear to ear, putting our backs into the fish as they ran out line. Little did we know that this action would continue nonstop for the next two hours, and Lord only knows how long these fish had been in the surf feeding before we arrived.

The fish were all stripers and there were very few that appeared to be less than 30 pounds. For a while, we were onto a bass with every cast and, since the regulations at that time allowed only one fish per fisherman per day, each one of us was thinking that he had better exercise patience and not be too hasty in picking a keeper, only to have to return a 50- or 60-pounder later. By the time the action stopped that morning, each one of us had released between 15 and 20 stripers in the 30- and 40-pound range. It was the most exhilarating fishing experience that any of the three of us have ever had. What is amazing is how large this school must have been and that there weren't more fishermen present to see it happen, especially in October, which is prime fishing time. The school of stripers had stretched at least another quarter of a mile around the cove point and to the east. I knew this because I could see the two guys from the truck whom we saw when we first arrived, and they were out on that particular point pulling in big bass with the same regularity as we were from the cove. Aside from us and the two other fishermen, there didn't seem to be anyone else around. Had there been others there, this blitz might have easily exceeded the Columbus Day blitz in terms of the total number of bass caught.

When the stripers finally moved out with the receding tide, Bruce and Raymond and I just sat on the rocks exhausted, looking at each other in amazement at what we had been lucky enough to experience. I had a 40-pound bass at my feet, Raymond had a 37-pound beauty and Bruce, a nice 28-pounder. To Bruce's credit, he would probably have had a much larger fish; however, he kept a smaller fish out of concern for its ultimate survival (if he had released it) because he noticed that one of his lure's treble hooks had damaged the fish's gills. When we went to pick up Bruce's father and uncle from the ferry later that afternoon, we tried to contain our excitement regarding our success until we could get them back to the house and present the fish, but they told us that they knew something was up — we were just way too smug in our manner. Of course you can probably guess where they wanted to fish later that evening — but the bass never came back. Not that evening. Not the next day. Is it any wonder how the famous saying so often heard in bait shops came into being? *You shoulda been here yesterday!*

**From left to right: Raymond Pettus, Leo Orsi and Bruce Shepley with some of the spoils from the Black Rock blitz of October 1993.**

As a final note, I've heard a lot of fisherman refer to the '60s and '70s as the "glory years" of striper fishing, when huge bass were caught with regularity and in record numbers, and in the same breath proclaiming that it would never happen like that again. I disagree. You so often hear this because people tend to forget that when you have a severe decline in the hatch for an extended number of years (as happened during the '60s and '70s), 20 years later, you will not have a large population of big bass (20 years is roughly the time required for a striper to reach between 45 and 50 pounds). It also follows that 20 years after a great young-of-the-year hatch (which happened in some years of the '80s), you will start to see many more bass in the 50-pound category being caught. We are now about 20 years out from several of the best hatches on record. As of the writing of this book, over 50 stripers that weighed 50 pounds or more had been reported in 2003 — a level that curiously coincides with the "glory years." Coincidence? I hope not.

I'll close this chapter with an excerpt from a fishing report that appeared in the Providence Journal in July of 2003:

*"In the history of Rhode Island striper fishing, no one can remember a day like that," Alan Gelfuso said of last Saturday off Southeast Light. "There were boats with two 40-pounders on at the same time," he said. Mike Fahey caught a 48-pound fish and a 51-pounder. Aboard the charter boat Adrianna, skipper Mike Neto guided Boon Robertson, 12, of West Virginia to a fish that weighed 63.05 pounds, a potential junior world record......." "Anglers that switched to wire line continued to catch fish all around the island," said Mattera of Kenport Marina. Larissa Wright caught a 45-pounder on a tube-and-worm rig, and Al Conti said he knows of at least five 50-pounders taken this week..."*

HOOD

# Chapter VIII

## Chronicles

*from*

## Legends, Old Timers & Seasoned Salts

There is no substitute for experience. The beginner fisherman could read 10 books about striped bass fishing and, although he might gain a solid understanding of the principles of the sport, without spending time in the surf he would still be a beginner. There can be no argument that spending night after night, year after year, casting into the surf improves one's ability and understanding of the sport far more than any book ever will. The surf's environment is nature's instructor and the fishermen who become graduates of her classroom are the genuine diehards — the ones who spend an enormous amount of time being slapped in the face by waves, soaked to the bone by rains, and chilled by driving winds — all necessary lessons on the path to becoming an accomplished surfcaster.

It is a very special sport that compels its participants to leave the comforts of their homes to brave the cold, the wind, and the rain, and usually to fish in the middle of the night, while most folks are snug in their beds under warm blankets. It is likewise a very special fisherman who shrugs off those conditions night after night after night, year after year after year, in pursuit of the fish. For most striped bass fishermen, being able to fish an average of just once or twice a week during the season would be an accomplishment. Many of us don't have enough opportunity to even come close to that. So imagine, if you will, a fisherman who has fished for striped bass on an average of 130 (almost consecutive) nights of each season and for the better part of 20 consecutive years. It would be a fair bet that the fisherman who had experienced such an incredible stint — more bass fishing in one season than most fishermen do in five years — might have some interesting experiences chronicled in his memory box. Such a fisherman is Frank Daignault, and such a fisherman is his wife, Joyce.

Frank and Joyce are two of New England's surf fishing legends. For 20 years or so, from June through early September and then weekends during the fall, while the commercial sale of striped bass was still legal, Frank and Joyce and their four children fished almost every night for stripers on Cape Cod. And no, they weren't staying in a condo on the beach; they were living all summer long in a small four-wheel-drive camper, and driving up and down the beach all night long in search of fish. They were all accomplished surf fishermen right down to their youngest daughter. In a combined effort, they would routinely land catches of up to 500 pounds of striped bass a night (sometimes much more).

Not all of Frank's fishing was done on the Cape, however. When I first started to make trips to Jamestown with Bruce Shepley, and during the second and third years that we fished the island, we noticed that a small group of guys was always fishing from the rails of the old Jamestown Bridge. One night when Bruce and I were driving over the bridge, we slowed down to see what they had caught, and when our headlights got within close proximity, we couldn't believe what we were seeing. Lying on the road next to the bridge's side rail were at least four bass that looked to be in the 30-pound class and just ahead was a guy walking off the bridge carrying a fish that was an easy 40 pounds! One of those guys was Frank Daignault. Frank and a few of his fishing buddies had discovered that depending upon the tide, the big stripers would set themselves up in the shadows of the bridge, where they would lie in wait, ready to ambush the baitfish being washed through by the current.

I caught up with Frank recently and asked him about his successes fishing from the Jamestown Bridge, and this is what he told me:

*"I would have to guess at it, but I think it was somewhere between '71 and '74. The biggest one that I've ever taken off of that bridge was 46 pounds. The reason that there were not more big fish taken is that most guys who fooled around out there had kind of given up on the notion of defeating the fish. What they would do was hook and fight the fish until they broke off. In trying to go ashore with them, everybody has to try it once to find out that it's impossible. It does something to the muscles along your kidneys — just above your belt, on the side? And it is so excruciating because you're forcing sideways — I can't explain it, but I know that I did it once with a 36-pounder and I got the fish, but I swear I'd never do it again! And I talked to other guys who had done it and they all said they would never do it again either."*

Frank and his buddies had finally figured out that there had to be a better way of dealing with these big fish rather than walking them nearly a half-mile down the bridge in order to reach the shore. So what they did was to devise a line gaff that consisted of nylon line attached to a very sharp four-pronged grappling hook. The line gaff was attached with another clip to the fishing line of the rod that had caught the fish and was then lowered off the side of the bridge to snag the fish. The specifications of the gaff had to be fairly precise; otherwise, the results would be far less than desired. On one occasion, for example, a fish fell off the gaff as it was being hoisted up, and, since the fisherman who had caught the fish had already closed the bail on his reel, the falling fish jerked the rod right out of his hands and off the side of the bridge.

*"I defeated the 46-pounder with that line gaff. I got a lot of other fish, too, that were in the 38- to 40-pound range. But what happened after a while was that we got hassled by the authorities, although I do think it was out of concern for our safety. When you fish the side of the bridge with no sidewalk, the big 20-ton trucks that are going by almost suck you into their afterburner. It was really scary."*

Not only was it scary, but it was also dangerous. Frank said that the most feared hazards were the drunks who would drive by at excessive speeds and throw beer bottles at the fishermen or, worse, lowlife drivers who would stop and try to steal his fish! Of course today the old Jamestown Bridge is closed and fishing from it is prohibited. But what a twist to striper fishing that must have been!

Frank and Joyce have few equals when it comes to the number of large fish that they caught over the many years they have fished for striped bass. They have landed an unconscionable number of stripers during their lifetime in the surf and, as might be expected, there were several times that Frank caught fish that weighed in over the "magic mark" — the 50-pound club. I don't know what it is about striped bass fishermen and the 50-pound benchmark, but in fishing circles, joining the 50-pound club is analogous to receiving the Academy Award for striped bass fishing. I asked Frank how many "Academy Awards" he had received:

*"Seven 50-pounders. The largest was 53 and the smallest was 50 and ounces. A lot of those were 52s. I got one in '64, one in '66, one in '67, two in '69, and then one in '77 and one in '78. That was the end of it. Most of them were taken on live eels. Two of them were taken on a 'loaded' junior Atom. There were a limited number of junior Atoms produced that had extra lead in them and wouldn't float. You could control the depth of the plug and you could add action by jerking it. I caught the one in '66 with it and then the following season I was living in a camper on East Beach with my family and I was fishing live eels on a regular basis. We were getting a lot of decent fish — a strong pick of very big fish from 35 to 45 pounds — that sort of thing. But again, I was a victim of jealousy and some sonofabitch let my eels go or stole them. I got in the back pond, as I did every evening — I'd put my waders on or I'd go barefoot in the back — and I'd get maybe eight or 10 eels and put 'em in a wet bank bag — a money bag — strap it around my waist and start doing the beach. I'd go until I was exhausted or, if the fishing was poor, I might quit at 2 or 3 a.m., but if it was good, I'd go till daybreak. So, as I was saying, my eels were taken from me. I had none in my box so I got back and I said, 'Geeze, now what do I do? I guess I'll have to plug.' I was very disappointed*

*because I believed, at the time, that the eel was the best thing. So I said, 'Hey, I'm gonna to put that loaded junior Atom on, the one that I got the 50-pounder on last October.' And within 20 minutes, I had another one! On the same plug! Yeah, so the night they got my eels, I got the 50-pounder.*

*"The one I got in '77, I was fishing North Truro on the ocean side, the back beach, and there were mostly big bass around, but we did have a sprinkling of bluefish. I was pumping a rigged eel and I got hit. I set on the fish and I didn't get him. I resumed pumping on it, but it didn't feel the same. It felt lighter because a bluefish had cut my eel off. So I said, 'I'll get that sonofabitch,' and I kept pumping it the rest of the retrieve and I got slammed. So I really socked the bastard cause now I got a half an eel so he should've gotten the hook. And I did hook him. But it was a 52-pound bass. And I looked inside the jaw of the fish and there was half an eel. All in the same cast!*

*"Let me add one thing. My wife had one 50-pounder. Fifty pounds, 6 ounces. And that's over the mantel in the living room right now. She got it in '77. When Joyce was fishing with me, I caught two 50-pounders and she caught one. In other words, if she'd been fishing with me the whole time, she might have gotten six or seven. You know what I'm saying?"*

Did you know Rebelle Felice, the past owner of the Creek Bait Shop on Jamestown?

*"Yes, I had only one experience with Rebelle, and it was memorable. It was about 1958. I had a 1-year-old baby. We left the baby with her mother, I think. Joyce had to be around 18 or 19 and I was around 22. We stopped over there* [at the bait shop] *and I asked* [Rebelle] *if he knew where we could catch some flounder. So he sold us some mummies, and then he says, 'Where's your boat?' And I said, 'Well, we don't have a boat.' 'Ah, Jesus,' he says, 'So I guess you don't have a motor?' 'No, I don't have a boat or a motor.' So he gave us his boat, which was pulled up on the beach at Mackerel Cove. It had an outboard motor, which he had to show me how to start, 'cause I had no clue. He told us to get out in the cove, shut the motor off, let the wind push us, and just drag bottom, right? So we filled the boat with fluke! Oh man, we cleaned up, it was like a dream! We ate fluke all summer. It was just incredible because Rebelle didn't know us from Adam and he loaned us his boat. It was a different time then — it was just great!"*

Everybody knows that no matter how much of an expert you are, you make mistakes while you are learning the ropes. It's easy to get caught up in the excitement of a great fishing moment and to forget to do the things that should be a matter of habit. Like the time I left my spare cooler full of fishing equipment on the ground at Southwest Point. I had caught some really nice bass, and I was so excited that I rushed back to make the ferry and forgot to take the cooler with me; someone ended up with some nice stuff. I asked

Frank if there were any similar moments in his repertoire of surf fishing adventures:

*"Well, we really did all the dumb things that everybody does when they start out fishing. I remember when we first started striper fishing, we had a contest for the season and I won it with a 4½-pound striper!*

*"The most perilous thing I did was to drive into Chatham Inlet in 11 feet of water at midnight. We were into fish, and I thought that because of the way the rods were going down the fish were comin' in from the sea and going into Pleasant Bay. So I said, 'Saddle up and let's get ahead of 'em'. I didn't want to put the headlights on and it was very foggy. It was the top of the tide so the water was level with the beach. I was driving in the dark and we just slid into 11 feet of water. We were lucky to get out alive — the water was coming in the windows. Joyce climbed out her side and I climbed out mine. That's probably the worst one.*

*"We also had a lot of very scary guys around who would get mad if you caught more fish than them and would pick a fight with you. I was pretty lucky; I only had one incident. The money caused it to happen. Don't forget that these fish were 40 pounds and they were bringing $2.50 a pound, so that's a hundred dollars a fish. In 1978, 1979 dollars, that was a lot of money."*

I guess that aside from a few mishaps and several jealous and disgruntled anglers, those were the "good old days"?

*"The 'good old days'? They were the bad old days. Today I drive cars that never need service. If you're old enough to remember the 'bad old days,' you had to have a carburetor and a fuel pump under the seat. If you were going to be a beach buggy jockey, you were forced to become some kind of a mechanic. And I'll tell you, I've changed a fuel pump with the sea washing into my face. We were having a moon tide and we were trying to move and the fuel pump quit. My wife held the flashlight while I was down in the sand changing a Goddammed fuel pump and the waves were breaking over the top of the beach into my face! And the no-seeums were biting me around my waist where my shirt came out. Yeah, the good old days — like hell!"*

What about Block Island? You did most of your fishing on the Cape and along the beaches of southern Rhode Island, but did you ever make it out to the Block?

*"The first article I ever published was in a summer issue of Saltwater Sportsman magazine in 1970. It was called 'Block Island Safari.' The article was about surfcasting for giant bluefish. The best bluefish we caught on Block Island were 10-pounders. Before that, the bluefish we caught were like 3 and 4 pounds when you could find 'em. They were considered an exotic species all through the '60s. Historically, the bluefish opportunity has never been very*

*constant. Just like striper populations — they're highly variable. What we did learn, and I made the point in the article, was that we were catching bluefish in the daytime on popping plugs which was really something! And then after catching bluefish all day, we were catching 18- to 20-pound stripers at night. This is at Block Island — which was not viewed as striper territory. And it was in July."*

Block Island wasn't viewed as striper territory?!

*"No, not really. I had never heard of anybody fishing there — they only went there for bluefish."*

So that was your first time out there fishing?

*"Yes. Our 11-year old son, Dick, was with me and he had a ball — we loved it. The stripers would school and we got 'em on swimming plugs. And on the south shore, right there at Mohegan Bluffs."*

At the bottom of the steps?

*"They didn't have steps then. It was all mountain goat stuff. I never went back because I thought that it was too much of a hassle when compared to what we could do on the south shore of Rhode Island. You had to pay to put the car on the ferry, and in 1970, I was conscious about the cost of everything."*

Frank is now 66 and has been retired from teaching for 14 years. He is still an avid fisherman and has authored six books and hundreds of articles for sports fishing magazines and journals. If you haven't read any of his books, you owe it to yourself to do so, especially "Eastern Tides" and "Twenty Years on the Cape." Those two books alone will amaze you with how one man and his family could catch so many striped bass and have experienced so many bass fishing adventures.

To be sure, striper fishing has changed considerably from the days when Frank and others like him roamed the surf every night. During the years when these men and women stayed up all night catching stripers along the entire New England coastline, they were able to sell their catch each morning to fish processors, who would pay a healthy price for the whole bass. The fish would then be shipped off to larger markets, such as New York City, where they were in high demand and would bring double or triple the prices paid to the fishermen. When the bass numbers slid into a disastrous decline during the early '80s, the commercial harvest of stripers by surfcasters came to an end. Today the fish is largely considered to have game-fish status, although commercial harvest by surfcasters does take place to a lesser extent, but only through a special license/permit and with harvest restrictions. By contrast, during the '60s and '70s it wasn't uncommon for a professional surf fisherman to earn a thousand dollars on a very good night. With most of the bass over 30 pounds, and the price at the scale running around $2 per pound for the whole fish, even a small handful of fish made for a good night.

Not long ago, Kevin Weaver, editor-at-large for the Block Island Times, published a three-part series in the weekly island newspaper titled "An Island Ringed by Striped Bass." The article provided some excellent insight into a very different era of striper fishing, at a time when the majority of the stripers caught on the Block were quite large. Such catches helped to supplement the incomes of a group of very good island fishermen. As part of the article, Kevin had interviewed some of the fishermen who were part of that local group of commercial surfcasters. I caught up with Kevin recently and asked if he would share some of the interview comments for the readers of the Chronicles, and he agreed. Here is part of what he wrote:

Twenty years ago, lobsterman Jon Grant earned extra income by surfcasting for striped bass. His annual two months of professional bass fishing was the stuff of legend: big catches, empty beaches and endless hours of surfcasting. Grant and his companions who fished in the 1980s were the last men to fish professionally for striped bass from Block Island beaches. They would begin fishing in the spring, but fished most intensively in the fall, when demand for the fish was higher. Grant consistently earned good money catching stripers in September and October, when the largest of the fish were migrating southward, past Block Island beaches toward warmer waters and inland spawning grounds.

*"We would fish all night, ship the fish off on the first ferry, sleep until about 3, then start checking the beaches again,"* Grant remembered. *"We practically lived in our cars."*

A good night would produce six to eight fish weighing 30 pounds or more.

*"Eighty dollars per night was a slow night. Fish taken to the market generally ranged from 22 to 45 pounds. Anything smaller was tossed back,"* explained Grant.

He recalled one good night of fishing;

*"I had 22 fish. I was fishing next to Steve Smith. He had 16. My biggest was 48 pounds. Steve's biggest was 64½ pounds. The rest were 30s and 40s, and we broke off just as many. That was a little Christmas present."*

*"Now people catch 20 fish in a night, but they're 10- to 15-pound fish. The fish are a lot smaller now, but there are a lot more of them."*

Other Block Islanders who were actively pursuing the bass along with Grant were Steve Smith, Tom Civil, Joe Fallon, Chris Littlefield, Steve Winters and Albert Littlefield. And there were generations of surf fishermen before Grant's time as well. Among them were Willis Dodge, Fred Benson, Omar Littlefield, Bill Phelan, Mart Conley and others.

Weaver also wrote that Grant and the other Block Island fishermen realize that they were fishing for bass at a special time in history.

*"We probably saw bass fishing at its pinnacle,"* said Charlie Dodge, another Block Islander casting for stripers in those days. *"The standard joke was that a Block Island schoolie was 36 pounds. We didn't catch little fish. That's when they got worried and put the brakes on it, because there were no young coming."*

What he sees now, he says, is *"beyond a big resurgence. It's hard not to catch one now. You see people who don't have a clue and they're pulling in fish after fish."*

**Commercial bass fisherman Steve Smith with one of his biggest catches of 1982.**

**John Grant and Steve Smith shipped this night's catch off-island on Nov. 26, 1982: 52 fish totaling 1,742 pounds.**

One bassman who clearly *does* have a clue and who has paid his dues in the Rhode Island and Massachusetts surf for over 40 years is veteran surfcaster and accomplished author Charley Soares. Charley has roamed the New England coastline fishing for stripers ever since he was a teenager — and my bet is that there are few avid striper fishermen that haven't read and appreciated at least one of Charley's articles or documentaries, which appear frequently in The Fisherman and/or On The Water magazines. I spoke with Charley recently and I asked him how he became interested in this great sport and also if he would be kind enough to share some of his own chronicles with me. Here's some of what he had to say:

*"I grew up in Massachusetts, and right around the time my father died in '53, when I was in high school, I used to run errands for a group of*

*real crusty old-timers at the Weetamoe Yacht Club. And that sounds kinda fancy, but it was actually a blue-collar boat club, which was one of the first incorporated boat clubs of its kind in the country. It was in Fall River Massachusetts on the bank of the Taunton River. My reward for the errands would be that sometimes I got to go fishing with these guys.*

*"I also used to row these guys around in a skiff while they would fish. The basic bait in those days was the sea worm, which I dug myself, and would sell to them for 10 cents a dozen. And most of these guys fished with hand lines, which were about 27-pound test. The problem with that type of fishing was that most of the time they wrapped the line around their hand. I lost the feeling in my right hand once because I had a big fish that turned the 12-foot skiff around. I had* [caught] *him on a Cape Cod Spinner and I knew that if I tried to stop the fish I would break the line so I kinda just let the fish take the boat."*

So you were already sort of a striper guide as a teenager?

*"Yeah, I would bring these guys to the places where we caught these fish and some of the rich guys who had Ocean City spinning reels would cast popping plugs into the rips. I remember one of the hottest plugs at the time was the Pflueger Minnow, which used to cost about 79 cents each.*

*"And there were a lot of fish around in those days too. So often the plug would hit the water and only have to move three or four feet before it would have a bass after it. And so these guys looked at me like I walked on water, but all I was doing was just following what I saw other people do."*

Where did you guys like to fish?

*"We fished on the Cape. We fished along Buzzards Bay. And a tremendous amount of fishing that we did from the surf was off Newport and Jamestown. At one point, I fished about six years almost every night* [during the season] *and I'm still paying the price for it right now* [he said while laughing]. *My friend Russell and I would work all day and then we would fish all night. We marketed the fish that we caught at F. B. Drake the next day. We'd get back to the house at 2 or 3 in the morning, take a bath, go to bed, and then wake up at 5 in the morning to drive to Providence to go to work. When Newport started to get very crowded, we started fishing Jamestown. We fished Beavertail. We fished Mackerel Cove, we fished around the old bass stands and over on the west side in back of Fort Getty.*

*"We fished from the rocks of Newport and Jamestown. Having no understanding of what the old bass stands were, we just called them 'the pipes,' not knowing that some wealthy man had paid someone to drill some holes in the rocks to insert the pipes to make a walkway that got him out to where he could catch big fish. In fact, there was a name on one of them — I think it said 'Property of Clarence Riley,' eighteen hundred and something."*

So you guys figured that if someone went through the trouble to erect a stand at a particular spot, there must be a good reason to fish there?

*"Absolutely! There was usually whitewater on either side and a hole in front where the water was fairly still and that's where the big bass would lay and wait for the baitfish to get tossed around."*

When did you start writing about fishing?

*"In 1958, when I became the fishing committee chairman for the Linesiders Bass Club which competed in the R.J. Schaeffer Saltwater Fishing Contest. I sent one of my first stories to Frank Woolner* [an editor emeritus of Saltwater Sportsman magazine] *in the spring of '64 and he sent me a letter back that said, 'I'm going to buy the story,' and he paid me more for that story than I was making in a week with my other jobs!"*

You mentioned the R.J. Schaeffer Contest — that contest was a big deal during those days wasn't it?

*"There were about 350 clubs in nine or 10 states and at one point there were about 40,000 anglers competing. In fact, in June of 1964, I caught a 58-pound bass and there were 37 other 50-pounders that were entered by various other clubs. But I got beat out by a member of my own club, Herb Dickinson, who was a friend of mine and who I often fished with. Herb caught a 64-pounder!*

*"I don't think that fishing [today or in the future] will ever get to be as good as it was in the '60s. Those were the glory years. There were just so many more huge fish then and a better spread of year-classes. For instance, during those years we had a catch one night that included four 50-pound bass out of a catch of 37 fish. We caught over 1,300 pounds of fish that night on live eels and we did it legally, because at that time, the managers thought that the striped bass resource was healthy."*

What about the Block? Did you ever fish out there?

*"Yes, I did some fishing out there. I went with Tim Coleman* [also an editor with The Fisherman magazine] *and some of his friends who used to rent a cottage on Block Island every year during November when most people thought that all the fish had already left. They found out about the Block because some guy from the island told Tim that he had seen a fish that must have been 80 pounds. We all laughed when we heard that, but the guy said, 'Tim, I know bass and I catch fish. And the guy that caught this fish also catches fish all the time and he never says a word to anybody, but I saw him*

*putting this fish in the back of his truck and the tail on the fish was twice as wide as any 40-pounder I ever saw.' And let me tell you, it was easier to get nuclear secrets from the Russians than it was to get information about striped bass fishing and hot spots in those days. That's the way it was.*

*"So Tim used to leave an old Oldsmobile station wagon out on the island to drive to places where we would slide down the banks* [to get to the water]. *He and his group were very kind to me and invited me to join them occasionally out on the Block. One night, Tim caught two 50s and a 67-pounder on a Danny needlefish! That Block Island fishing was some of the most fantastic fishing in the world at the time. They had a bonanza over there. And if that wasn't enough, just imagine this — Tim told me, 'Charley, in hindsight, I would give back all the big fish that I have caught just to see the ones that I lost.'"*

Spending so much time fishing over the years, and knowing that stormy conditions will usually bring some of the best fishing, we've all had some harrowing experiences trying to balance good (safe) fishing and turbulent waters — do any of your challenges come to mind?

*"There's a place called Minister's Rock. It's called that because in the very early days of Little Compton, there wasn't a church. So a minister would get up on this big boulder next to the water on Sundays and people would gather around on blankets to hear his sermon. It's in a big cove and the southwest wind blows right in there.*

*We fished off of this rock often and in fact, my friend Russell eventually caught at least seven or eight 50-pounders from there. Unfortunately, I never once did — I was the bridesmaid on this rock. Well, we were on this rock during the night of a very serious storm, when we should not have been there. We were taking water up to our knees from the waves coming up over the rock. Suddenly, one huge wave came over. It washed away my army knapsack, which was full of lead sinkers and other heavy things, and knocked me down as well — and I had hip boots on because you needed them to wade out there. Russell was able to fall backwards and hang onto his rod, but I lost my rod and reel, I split my chin, busted my nose, and we were very lucky to come out of that alive. We should not have been on that rock that night. We also lost all the fish that we had caught. We had at least four fish in the 25- to 35-pound class that were all tied together and to the knapsack, and we lost everything. We looked at each other, and although we were very disappointed to lose everything we had, we knew we were lucky to be left with our lives.*

*"In Newport and Jamestown, as you know, every year since I was born, there have been at least one or two tragedies each year where people get sucked off those rocks. And it's not so much that they drown, it's that they get their skulls beat in because they get pounded up against the rocks — and most*

*of them have waders on. You just have to realize that there are some real inherent dangers to certain aspects of this sport."*

Just as there are some close calls in the memory surf bags of most veteran surfcasters, there are some amusing moments.

*"Well, this is not amusing at all because I want to cry every time I think about it* [he said laughing]. *I never knew how to tie an improved clinch knot. You see, today, fishermen take so much for granted. They can pick up almost any* [fishing] *book and learn how to tie an improved clinch knot or an Albright knot. I didn't have any mentors that had any of those skills. The old-timers who I fished with tied their lures on with three double overhand knots. So with the knots that I was using* [at an early age], *when you got a big fish on and the line went slack, you prayed to God that the line was broken, because if the line came back in and there was a pigtail on the end of the leader, it meant that your knot unraveled or let go. And Leo, I can't tell you how many times I actually stood there with that line in my hand and with tears welling up in my eyes because I lost a big fish due to my inexperience in tying knots."*

Don't feel bad, Charley, so many of us have also discovered the meaning of that little curly pigtail at the end of a lure-less leader and the sinking feeling that comes along with it. Speaking of sinking feelings, have you ever landed a fish, pulled it high up on the rocks and away from the water to disengage the hooks only to discover that another fisherman was standing in your spot right after you unhooked it and returned to the water's edge?

*"There was a certain type of justice that was meted out in those days for fishermen that didn't understand the protocol. There was a great deal of respect for someone else's rights and you had to learn and know the etiquette of fishing — from the surf or from the boat. Like if you saw a guy catching fish, you gave him plenty of room unless he waved you over. If he waved you over, you thanked him and you returned the favor in some way, shape or form, but you never crowded anyone. At least, we never did that kinda thing anyway. And I don't like 'chunkin'* [using chunks of cut bait] *because very few, if any, fish are caught in the mouth when you're chunkin'. They're almost all gut-hooked and with that, the mortality of released fish is very high."*

So how many times have you been in the 50-pound club?

*"I have nine 50-pounders up to 58 pounds, 8 ounces. Most were caught on live eels or a reverse Atom plug."*

A distinguished accomplishment and one that is well deserved — not only because of the effort, but also because of Charley's love and appreciation for the sport and his devotion to preserving and managing the resource. Anyone who has an interest in an historical perspective of the legendary catches of bass in the 60- and 70-pound category will enjoy Charley's recent two-part series on the subject, which was published in The Fisherman and On The Water magazines just prior to the publication of this book. In fact, he makes the interesting point that with so many 50-pound fish being caught during the past few years, we may soon see the return of the monster bass of the glory years. I sure hope so.

A chapter discussing some of Rhode Island's surfcasting legends and seasoned salts should certainly include another bassman who has been on the surf scene for at least as long as I can remember, and then some — Joe Mollica. Joe was born in Providence and started fishing at the age of 5. During his early years he spent his summers in the Oakland Beach area of upper Narragansett Bay, fishing nearly every day from a small wooden skiff. When he was older and his family would go to Scarborough Beach for the day, Joe would have them drop him off at the rocks in Narragansett next to what is now the Coast Guard Restaurant and then pick him up at the end of the day. He wasn't interested in the beach — he wanted to fish. In the years following, Joe fished the mainland surf between Jamestown and across from Block Island for many years before he purchased and operated his own saltwater tackle shop, which was named Top of the Dock. That's where I first met Joe about 27 years ago, when he opened the shop in 1977. The shop was located in Narragansett on a hill just above what was then called Monahan's Dock and strategically overlooking the Narragansett coastline to the north. As you can probably imagine, there are plenty of interesting, amusing and sometimes sad stories that come in through the doors of a tackle shop and Joe's was no exception. I asked him about that recently.

*"When I owned the Top of the Dock, I saw a lot of mistakes right out at the boat ramp in front of the shop. We've seen cars, trucks and everything else go right in at that ramp. Slide right in the water, a brand-new vehicle, right up to the roof! We had one guy launch his little boat from the ramp and he fell out while in the process and the boat was going around in circles with his dog in it. There was also the time some customers from Philadelphia were launching their 20-foot boat from the ramp. There was a big blitz going on and they were in such a hurry to get to the fish that they somehow launched the boat into the water, still attached to the trailer — it came off the hitch on the car and everything went down off the ramp! We saw a lot of stuff like that."*

Your shop was very close to the Hazard Avenue rocks, which is a very good fishing area, but they call it Hazard Avenue for a reason – care to expand on that?

*"I got the fear of God put into me the hard way out there one time. Me and a friend went down to Hazard Avenue — out on that big high rock on the right that you have to jump over to. It was a very stormy day — which we love to fish, you know that. In nor'easters, you had to be out there, and the more miserable, the better. We got caught up in the hype of the blitz syndrome. There were bass and bluefish all over the place. We were so wrapped up in the fishing action that we weren't paying attention and we almost got taken off that rock by a huge wave. In fact, the backwash took all our tackle bags. There was another fella out there that reached out to help us off the rock and it's a good thing too, because I think with another wave we would've been gone.*

*"During my tenure at the Top of the Dock, 14 people lost their lives off those rocks! And I was there 10 years. Unfortunately, one incident was a mother and her son."*

Are there any coastal areas in Rhode Island that you really consider to be personal favorites for fishing?

*"Definitely! The eastern coast of Naragansett from the Narrow River to Point Judith Light, and all the way down to Galilee, East Matunuck and Matunuck. Those are the areas where I spent most of my time crawling around on the rocks. Many years ago, you were able to access the mouth of the* [Narrow] *River from the north side. You could just walk out on the rocks; you didn't have to walk down the town beach. We spent many, many, many nights fishing there. We fished according to the tides and location, and we'd just plan a night and say, well ok, at high tide we ought to be on the rocks at Galilee, at midtide we'd go to Scarborough* [Beach] *and then we'd catch the latter part of the tide at the Town Beach. There was enough fishing in Narragansett that we rarely had to go anywhere else. My shop was located near a little place called The Gardens, which was just north of Hazard Avenue. You very rarely had to walk further from my shop than to Hazard Avenue and you had all the fishing you wanted."*

Did you do any fishing over on Block Island?

*"My God, we've had some great times at Grove Point on Block Island. One of our club members brought his son out for the first time on Block Island and he had made him a red needlefish, you know, homemade. I think at the time his son was about 13 or 14. After about 20 minutes, this kid had taken a fish that was over 60 pounds, as I recall. His first bass! And I wanted to drown him! Yeah, everything from then on was a let-down for this kid.*

*"I've also had occasions at Southwest Point on Block Island, very, very late in the season — early December — when the fish were all massive and your hands were so cold that is was really tough to bring ' em* [the fish]

*in. We'd only land one out of every five fish, but they were all big fish and they were hungry because they were leaving, you know?*

*"I think the needlefish* [plug] *came into its own on Block Island. I remember during the heydays going out there with other club members, and I used to bring cases of needlefish because at that time, Swienton* [at the Twin Maples tackle shop] *didn't even have them."*

Today, Joe is considered to be one of the best in Rhode Island at building custom surf rods and repairing reels. I asked him how he became so accomplished at these skills.

*"I used to perform my own maintenance on reels, like a lot of guys did, and I learned how to wrap a guide and to repair a guide; however, I was not into rod building and reel repair. When I bought the shop, the customers brought me reels that were disassembled in coffee cans! So I thought to myself, if you're gonna learn, this is how you're gonna learn. I also had some of the best mentors — old-timers — that were the former surfcasting generation; these were guys who had fished during the World War II era. They took me under their wing and really, I have to say, they were the ones that taught me. They were really good guys and superior surfcasters. They used 10-foot rods with only three spinning guides, which, of course, would be frowned upon now when you see all the guides that they wrap on today's rods — they make ' em with eight and nine guides! I don't know how many* [rods] *I built with just three guides and they worked great – nobody broke lines and everybody caught fish. Today it's considered rare, you know, you gotta have some scientific approach. Everybody has a mathematical equation to put guides on the rod.... in the old days, we'd find the spine, put the guides on, line ' em up, and it worked fine. To this day, I build rods for all the grandchildren of the guys that I built rods for back then, and I pretty much use the same system, only with four guides instead of three."*

Well, speaking of tried-and-true methods and systems, one of the reels that seems to have withstood the test of time is the Penn line.

*"Oh, definitely. The Penn 704 sort of evolved out of the old Ocean City and Shakespeare reels which preceded it — and it used to be that there wasn't a guy in Narragansett who didn't have one of those green reels. We used to call it the M-1 rifle of fishing reels."*

While we're on the subject of equipment, tell me something: If you had your choice of four plugs for surfcasting and couldn't use anything else for the rest of your life, what would you choose?

*"On the surface? I would choose an Atom popper. I don't know how long it's been around — my guess is 40 years or better and it's still one of the most effective plugs there is. I love the plug and I still use it. The next plugs I would choose are the Atom swimmer and the Danny swimmer. It* [the Danny] *casts like crap, but if you got that plug into some rough water where there were fish, it was just a matter of time before you hooked up. And that's a plug that's disappeared — there are replicas, but the original Danny's gone. The fourth plug would be of the newer generation, if you will, and that's the needlefish."*

Having owned a bait-and-tackle shop for so many years, you must have seen some remarkable catches come to the scale.

"*Well, the biggest I've ever caught was 48½ pounds and I'm so sorry that I never had it mounted. I've never caught a 50. There's one guy though, his name is John Martini — he's caught close to 60 bass over 50 pounds! Over years and years of fishing, and you know what? He has never caught one over 60!*"

I should have such a problem.

However, hearing this, I just had to speak with John Martini. Catching one striper of 50 pounds is considered by most East Coast fishermen as a lifetime accomplishment — the Academy Award of surfcasting. Catching seven or nine, or even a dozen 50-pounders is simply amazing. But 60?! Well, sure enough, I caught up with John Martini, and this is what he told me:

"I've *caught 59 of 'em — all 50 pounders. I got my first one in 1967 and I got my last one two years ago, so over a period of about 37 years, I guess. My biggest fish was 58 pounds."*

Well, I know better than to ask for your secret spots, but is there any general area that you find particularly productive?

*"I caught a few of these fish in Massachusetts, but most are from Rhode Island. I fish around Block Island all the time, and in fact, the big majority of these fish came from Block Island."*

Really?! Do you fish exclusively at night?

*"Yes, I used to, but over the last six or seven years, I fished during the day because I'm retired now and I can go during the day. I haven't night-fished in quite a while; however, most of my fish in prior years were caught at night. I strictly use eels, although sometimes in the spring I like to use herring,*

*but that's a lot of work. I can catch ' em* [the big bass] *on eels during the day — they'll hit the eels during the day — don't let anybody tell you any different. You don't have to exclusively fish at night. I cast the eels along the beach from my boat. In fact, all these fish were caught from a boat."*

So what's the secret to catching so many huge bass?

*"I always tell everybody, I don't do anything different or secret to catch big fish. The simple fact is that if you put the time in and the fish are there, you're gonna catch 'em — and I fished almost every night* [of the season]. *That's the secret. If you're out a lot, the chances of getting the big fish when they show up are very good — you're gonna get 'em. There's no secret lure, there's no secret bait — it's time spent on the water.*

*"I've always had the best luck out at the island in July and late November. The first two weeks of July and when the new moon comes in November, that's when you gotta start fishing. I like the first sliver of the moon; I've had a lot of luck on the first sliver."*

Is there any single catch that particularly stands out in your mind?

*"Well, in 1985, me and my partner got four 50-pounders in one night. In fact, I did that twice — once at Block Island and once at Cuttyhunk."*

Is there anything else you'd like to add?

*"Well, there's this friend of mine, his name is Danny Zubeck, and he's from Connecticut. He's around 80 years old now and he's caught about 100 bass of 50 pounds or greater. He's my hero."*

I can't even begin to imagine.

Finally, this chapter simply wouldn't be complete without mentioning one of the most legendary striper catches — and the current Rhode Island State record — Joe Szabo's 70½-pounder, which was caught on November 28, 1984, from the shores of — where else? — The Block, of course.

Joe has been a Block Island resident for about 23 years and he starting fishing the island's shorelines even before that. It was Thanksgiving week when Joe landed the state trophy — he was fishing with his father and another friend that evening.

*"It was the week of the full moon and we had driven around all over the island that night, probably 25 or 30 miles, just stoppin' makin' a few casts, moving again and just looking for something to work on. I remember my dad*

*saying, 'When are you going to take me to the place where you take your friends?' Actually, I wanted to throw him out of the car by that time.*

*"We ended up at Southwest Point and there was no one else there — and there were a lot of people on the island fishin' that night. In fact, my dad wanted to move and I said, 'You know, we caught some nice fish in here the last time we were here, and there's no one here'..... my dad was quite the character, to be honest with you. He told my mom that the record fish should have been his fish because I made him go get some cold beer out of the truck and that's the reason he didn't catch it. At the time, we were arguing about who was gonna go get the beer.*

*"So I said, 'Well, you know, we've got two currents coming across one another here and if we're gonna get into any fish, it's gonna be right here.' And it was blowin' real hard that night — the surf was crackin'— we had a storm or something offshore. The ocean was horrendous. Most guys wouldn't have fished it, but that's where you want to be. Where the ocean is the craziest is where the fish are going to be.*

*"The wind was coming off the top of the island so we were out of the wind, but the wind was standing the ocean up and when I flipped the eel* [to cast it out into the surf], *I had to stop it* [from going too far] *because the wind had caught it and it was just going and going and going. When I stopped it, I felt a little bump, so I set and reeled, but I didn't know that I had the fish on until I got it right in front of me and it held there in the surf for almost 15 minutes (and that was on 17-pound test too). Finally, I got her in on a wave and I thought it was the most exciting thing ever — I was yelling, 'Yahoo! Yahoo!' My father thought that I had hurt myself or something. He was way up on top of the hill and he came charging down to look at it. It must be 60 pounds, I kept saying to myself. We weighed it later that night on a bathroom scale and then the next morning I weighed it in on a couple different scales over at Swienton's* [Twin Maples]. *It was actually 70½ pounds the next morning, so the fish was probably 4 or 5 pounds bigger before the dehydration because I just threw it in the back of the pickup, you know?*

*"Actually, the ex-governor of Rhode Island, Phil Noel, was there. He was also fishing that night, but in a different location. He was the one who talked me into weighing it in to see if it was a record, because at first, I didn't realize it was a record."*

I know that was the biggest bass that you've ever caught, but had you caught many big fish up until that point and afterwards?

*"Oh, I have somewhere around 10 50-pounders. I caught five fish that year that were over 50 pounds. That was probably the last year of the real big fish."*

At the printing of this book, Joe's record still stands, and at 70½ pounds, it's going to be a tough one to beat. If you'd like to see what it will take to get your own name in the state record book, you can see Joe's fish, which has been mounted and is on display at Rebecca's Restaurant at the top of Water Street on the Block. It's an inspiration, to say the least.

**Joe Szabo and son with Joe's Rhode Island State Record 70½-pound striped bass.**

# Chapter IX

## The Dark,

## The Day the Cows Came Home
## &
## A New Meaning to "Getting Skunked"

By and large, success in fishing for stripers increases exponentially when you fish at night. The creatures are, by nature, nocturnal predators and as any seasoned bass fisherman will tell you, they really do come out at night. I've heard all sorts of theories as to why these fish lose their fear of — or sensitivity to — being in close to shore when there's no light, but as Frank Daignault would say, it sounds like a lot of "junk science" to me. Fishermen, on the other hand, weren't exactly engineered for the night foray. We weren't blessed with cat's eyes, we don't have cat-balance (I swear the rocks are more slippery at night), and there's just something about the prospect of falling in the water *at night* that takes on a whole new significance. If you're a beach fisherman, you're probably wondering why I'm making such a big deal about fishing at night. After all, on the beaches of Narragansett, Charleston, or even the Cape, fishing the surf only requires a smooth walk over the sand. And in many places on the Cape, you can drive your vehicle right up to the spot on the beach where you wish to fish — kind of cushy if you ask me. Not so on Jamestown or out on the Block. Sure, there are a few places with sand beaches like Mackerel Cove in Jamestown or Sandy Point, Mansion Beach, and Charleston Beach on Block Island. But, for the most part, fishing on these two islands requires either standing on, walking over, or the outright scaling of cliffs, rocks, and boulders of various sizes and degrees of slipperiness. Flashlight or not, doing it at night doesn't make it any easier. And as far as using a flashlight is concerned, my gut feeling has always been that it's not a great idea to shine bright lights around the area that you're going to fish because it will spook the fish and quickly send them fleeing from the light source. At least that's the most widely held theory. Then again, I guess none of us really know what the fish are thinking. I have to chuckle at writers who say "the fish think this" and "the fish think that." Other than a fish probably thinking that its "goose was cooked" as I pulled it up on the beach, I can't tell you what the fish think (although I have been known to talk *to* them on occasion — they never listen as far as I can tell).

I've always considered it to be a good idea to be as stealthy as possible in your approach to the area you've selected to fish, so lighting up the shoreline with a 500,000-candle power searchlight would not be recommended. Don't laugh — it actually happened once. I was fishing below the Southeast Lighthouse on the Block one night with Bruce and Raymond. We hadn't been there very long when we noticed four bright lights shining down on the beach from the stairs at the top of the 150-foot bluff. At first, we thought it must have been some kids playing around, but the lights started to make their way down the stairs. They were shining haphazardly in all directions, including out into the water, and beaming in on everything along the beach — present company included. When the light brigade reached the beach, we discovered that it was a group of four fishermen who had come down to fish. They were equipped with heavy-duty searchlights (which were powerful enough to be seen from Long Island) and two Coleman gas lanterns. With their arrival, the beach was as bright as a ball field lit up for night play. Seeing this, Raymond, Bruce, and I decided it was time for a new fishing spot, especially since we weren't catching anything anyway — and the odds had suddenly gotten a whole lot worse. These guys weren't intentionally discourteous; they just didn't know any better. Raymond has coined a name for fishermen in this category; he calls them "ginkers." A ginker is someone who has bought himself the finest equipment, gadgets, gear, clothes, and all the newest fishing stuff that money can buy, but hasn't a clue how to use any of it. These were indeed the guys from Ginkerville.

If you've never fished at night, you'll find that casting into the dark takes a little getting used to. When you cast at night, you can't see where your plug goes, you can't see when it hits the water, and it's difficult to tell when it's almost back to shore after being reeled in. The experts recommend practicing your night techniques during the day by casting with your eyes closed. At the end of each cast, open your eyes and see if the plug landed where you thought it did. At first, your perception is usually way off, but it doesn't take long to get the hang of it.

The second skill to master is learning to sense, at the end of your retrieve, when your plug is close enough to lift out of the water and cast again. This is important for two reasons. First, it will help you to avoid getting snagged in the rocks and weeds that are close to the surface in the shallow surf line, and second, knowing the location of your plug is important in deciding how hard to set the hooks when you get a strike. The rationale is that if you're using monofilament line, and you get a strike at the far end of your cast, there's a lot of line out between you and the fish, and possibly a slight bow in the line if you're fishing in the wind. As a consequence, you'll have to slam the rod back pretty hard in order to achieve a good hook-set. In fact, sometimes it's even a good idea to reel the line in quickly at the same time you take the rod back until you feel a solid hookup. If, on the other hand, a fish strikes you close to shore, which is close to the end of your retrieve, there's very little line between you and the fish, and the connection will be direct and immediate. If you set the hook with the same fervor and determination as you would in the first situation, you will probably pull the hooks right out of the fish's mouth, or else end up with only a pair of fish lips on the end of your lure.

There's another good reason why, at night, you should learn how to sense when your plug gets close to you at the end of your retrieve — and I'm almost embarrassed to tell you this because it still happens to me sometimes when my concentration wanders off into the night. As your plug gets closer to shore on your retrieve, the likelihood of it bumping a rock or a weed increases as the water becomes shallower. Every once in a while, one of these "bumps" feels remarkably like a strike from a fish. When this happens, and if your plug is very close to you, as you slam your rod back for a good hook-set, you may find (but you won't see) your plug and all of its six or nine hooks sailing back at you at warp speed, only to have it hit you smack in the chest or somewhere worse. Unfortunately, there's no way to teach someone exactly how to know where his plug is at night because it's simply a matter of "feel." Experienced surfcasters will all tell you that the plug just feels different on the end of the rod when it's close to you as opposed to when it's farther out in the surf. After fishing with a plug for many years, most fishermen become so sensitive to the way the plug feels in the water that they can tell when it has snagged even the smallest piece of weed because it just doesn't feel right on the end of the rod.

Fishing alone at night is a very special experience and it offers a variety of different sensations, not the least of which is the mystique of the dark. When I first started fishing for striped bass on Block Island, the island's huge bluffs and jagged rocky shoreline were very imposing sights to a young surf fisherman — and that was during the day. During the first few years of learning the Block, I made many trips out to the island by myself and to say that I was slightly nervous about fishing alone, at night, in the big surf under the giant cliffs, would be a gross understatement.

From my perspective, there are three types of dark. There are the moonlit nights during the various phases of the moon. These are the lightest nights, so that with a cloudless sky, and adjusted eyes, you can see a fair distance. In fact, on a clear night with a full moon, it is possible to walk the entire shoreline unaided by any other light source. As desirable as that sounds, I'm in the camp that ascribes to the theory that you're basically wasting your time fishing under the bright light of the full moon — not that you won't ever catch a fish, but it's never been a very productive scenario for me. Then there's fishing on the moonless nights — very dark, but with more light than you might expect due, supposedly, to the diffusion of light from the island lights and also from the distant light emanating from the mainland. During those nights, fishing has historically been quite productive. Finally, there is the blackest of nights — the nights when the island is shrouded in fog or completely cloud-covered. There is nothing so pitch-black as the dead of night accompanied by a blanket of thick sea fog. On nights like those, not even your flashlight will penetrate the darkness for more than a few feet. You can't see where you are, you can't see where you came from, and you can't see where you're going.

It was a similar fog-shrouded night that I selected for one of my first solo fishing experiences on the Block. It was early June, and I had made the trip over to Block Island for a long weekend of spring fishing. In the spring, the island is particularly prone to becoming fog-bound because the temperature of the ocean surrounding the island is usually much cooler than the air temperature. When this happens, and if there's significant moisture present in the air, it frequently results in a fog shroud that is, as they say, "thick as pea soup." This was the case on that June day when I arrived on the Block, and I welcomed the conditions enthusiastically because just as the night enhances the striper bite, so too, does fog and cloud cover for fishing during the daytime. I caught a lot of bluefish that day, but as evening arrived, I decided that I would not be overly adventurous in the fog and attempt to scale down any of the steep cliffs found at several of the island's prized fishing spots — instead I elected to use the stairs next to the Southeast Lighthouse. When I arrived at the parking area above the stairs, the fog was so thick that I had to strain my eyes just to see if there were any other fishermen's cars or trucks in the parking lot — there were not. In a way, I guess I was sort of hoping that I wouldn't be alone in this black, eerie, sound-muting blanket of fog 150 feet below the bluff-top. But as so often is the case with springtime fishing on the Block, there are usually far fewer fishermen who fish the spring season than fish in the fall.

I will never forget fishing that night on the beach below the bluffs; it was so dark, and so mysterious. Today, I wouldn't even give it a second thought — I actually enjoy the rapturous embrace of night fog. But as a first experience for a young striper fisherman, I could hardly keep my mind on fishing that night. When you find yourself alone in this imposing environment for the first few times, all sorts of things tend to go through your mind, not the least of which is that you're being watched by someone, or some animal, or even by the austere cliffs behind you that somehow seem to glare down upon you. Nelson Bryant, distinguished outdoors editor for The New York Times, wrote about the same sensation in one of his short stories. He described standing at the water's edge in the black of night, casting repeatedly until almost mesmerized by the mysterious cliffs that would seem to take on the shape of menacing faces and objects — been there, done that — I couldn't agree more.

Most dedicated surf fishermen who have fished the night surf for many years will tell you that you soon become accustomed to the dark and begin to appreciate and desire the peacefulness and the solitude that accompanies it. As dusk falls, the sunbathers and the beach strollers disappear from the shorelines, leaving them once again as the surfcaster's sanctuary. One evening in early September, I was out fishing during the middle of the night and standing on the end of a sand spit at Sandy Point, casting into a calm surf that was more like a lake than an ocean. As the light breeze blew the scent of the island's fireplaces in my direction, I noticed that in the surf that was gently lapping at my feet there was an incredible line of phosphorescent organisms. Every time a small wave broke across the bar, the entire surf-line lit up like a neon sign against the dark moonless sky. It's nights like this that make you happy that you're a surfcaster, for as the rest of the world sleeps, God has given you a front-row seat to the best show on earth.

Once you become accustomed to the dark, there are plenty of other things you might encounter during a night's fishing expedition — some expected and some not. One such encounter can occur when you move from one fishing spot to another along the island roadways. With the roads desolate during the wee hours of the morning, the temptation to zoom around the island to the next fishing spot is all too inviting, especially with the absence of tourists, bicycles, and mopeds. Unfortunately, there is a large group of *other* island residents that are also on the prowl during the night — the deer. Over the past 10 years or so, the deer populations on both Jamestown and Block Island have grown tremendously — especially on the Block. In fact, there are so many deer on the "pork chop" that they sometimes find it necessary to reduce the herd size by hiring a sharpshooter. I don't agree with that method, but that's not a subject for this book. For those of you who would raise the argument that the deer were there first — they weren't. They were brought out to the Block by some of the early islanders many years ago. The concern for fishermen is obvious, especially on foggy nights late in the fall when the deer seem to have little fear of walking down the middle of the roadways. It's going to be interesting to see how the plight (or salvation) of the island deer eventually materializes because last year, a report was published that cited the possibility that the Block Island deer have evolved into a separate and distinct species. If that turns out to be the case, the deer could be considered to be a rare and endangered species and consequently protected from harvest. In any case, it looks as though there will be plenty of deer on both islands for the foreseeable future, so unless you're out of venison and you're looking to stock up the hard way, keep a watchful eye out on the late-night road or you might be filleting something you hadn't planned to — then again, as some of the islanders have been known to do...... (Well.... I'm not going there).

Speaking of dark and fog, this is a funny story that I always said I would tell one day. If you've never experienced pea soup fog, you might have difficulty understanding how it could be so thick that you couldn't see more than a few feet in front of you. Trust me, it's paralyzing — even during the day. We had one of those days a few years back when a group of us were out on Block Island fishing for the week. We were staying at Harvey's place on Southwest Point, and the fog had rolled in during the previous night producing a blanket so thick that it was almost impossible to drive — especially at night. Realizing that it would be entirely dangerous to make our way around the island that evening, we scrapped that idea and just fished the Point in front of the house after dinner. The next day, Harvey and several of his friends were coming out to the island and we had to pick up another vehicle from the house of one of his friends in order to accommodate everyone. Harvey's friend, Eliot, lived only a quarter of a mile away from Harvey and just off the main road, so Raymond, Bruce, and I decided to take care of this little task, first thing the next morning. We hopped in the truck and slowly inched our way along Southwest Road through the incredibly dense fog, which seemed to have become even more dense with the onset of the morning. It was quite dangerous and, even though we were proceeding at a crawl, if another vehicle had been coming from the opposite direction at any reasonable speed, there would have been no time for either of us to react. When we finally made it into the driveway of Eliot's house, we inched our way in the truck to where we assumed the other truck was parked. Bruce was the first to notice a blurry object in front of us and he suggested that we stop and figure out where things were in the yard before we hit or ran over something. It was a prophetic suggestion.

We all started to get out of the truck to have a look around. I was out of the truck first and had started to walk in front of it when, suddenly, as if a window were instantly cut out of the fog, I found myself staring, face to face, at the head of a 2,000-pound steer! This was apparently the blurry object that Bruce had detected in the distance. The head on this animal was easily 3 feet across — well, it sure looked that big to me — and it was certainly not what I was expecting to literally *pop out* of the fog. Unbeknown to the three of us, several steers had escaped from a nearby farm that morning and were roaming, undetected, around the yards of some of the island homes while munching on the tender lawn grass. This massive beast had scared the living daylights out of all of us, but I assure you, my perspective was just short of panic. Raymond and Bruce weren't staring up the animal's nostrils — I was. As luck would have it, the steer, sensing that it was not where it was supposed to be, and perhaps thinking that it had stumbled upon its owner trying to recapture it, lurched backwards into the fog only to smack directly into another of the 2,000-pound bovine escapees. This caused it and the rest of the animals to immediately panic and run. The problem was that they couldn't see where they were going, and although we couldn't see them either, we could hear all kinds of stuff breaking and smashing down as the stampede left the yard. We all had a good laugh and we were just thankful that they took off in the opposite direction and not toward us. I guess the moral of the story is don't ever tell anyone that you'll fish "till the cows come home," because on the Block, they just might.

You see some pretty amazing things when you spend a lot of time fishing and walking the coastline — some things you wouldn't believe unless you saw them with your own eyes. Such an event occurred a few years back and would certainly seem to fall into that category. I didn't see it firsthand, but considering the source, I believe it just the same. I was out on the Block in late September and I had entered the first annual fall fishing tournament sponsored by Block Island Fishworks, one of the local fly fishing shops. The tournament started on a Friday afternoon just as an approaching cold front hit the island. The best bass I managed to catch before the front hit was only slightly over 12 pounds. I kept it, but I was certain it wouldn't be a contender — more likely dinner.

Around midnight that Friday evening, the cold front brought in 40-knot winds and driving rain. The weather system shut down the fishing for the rest of the weekend. First prize in the tournament went to a bass that only weighed about 15 pounds and I think that my 12-pounder ended up in second or third place — a paltry showing for an island that is well known for its huge bass. Before I left the island, I had called Mary Stover, one of the local island realtors, to confirm arrangements for an upcoming rental. When I explained that I was on the island to fish the tournament, she laughed and said that her husband almost won the bass division of the tournament, but that he had actually gotten "skunked." I remember thinking, "How's that again?" She told me that he wanted to enter a striper that weighed about 40 pounds, but the fish wouldn't qualify because of the way he got it. Well, I was all ears to hear the next part. Turns out that he was fishing down at Black Rock in the tropical storm-like winds when lo and behold, a 40-pound bass washes up in the surf at his feet! The bass had something protruding from its mouth, which, upon closer inspection, turned out to be a large bluefish!! The striper had apparently tried to swallow a bluefish that was too big for it to handle and, in the process, the bluefish ended up getting stuck. The bluefish blocked the water flow through the striper's gills so both fish died and washed ashore together in the heavy surf. Fish entered into the tournament were required to actually *be caught* with a rod and reel — not by hand. So Mary's husband was out of luck. Well, sort of. I suspect those grilled striper fillets tasted just fine.

One of the terms that is used to describe a bad day of fishing is getting "skunked." Unfortunately, most fishermen have experienced being skunked at one time or other — such is the nature of the sport. Some of the old-timers still carry on the superstitious practice of not washing down their boats after a fabulous day of fishing so as not to wash the success off the boat. Likewise, upon returning to the dock after a day of getting skunked, they can't bring the hose out fast enough to "wash the skunk off the boat." Like stripers, skunks are primarily nocturnal animals, feeding at night and sleeping during the day. With all the miles of walking that I have put in along the Block Island coastline at night, I have never once seen a skunk. Nor have I smelled a skunk anywhere on the interior of the island. My theory is that skunks have never made it out to the Block, although I have no concrete evidence to support this other than never having seen or smelled one there.

However, being skunked on Jamestown can take on an entirely different and far less desirable connotation than not having caught any fish. Conanicut Island has been loaded with the little black-and-white-striped creatures for as long as I can remember. In fact, I have reached the point where the faint smell of skunk is an association synonymous with being on the island for a fishing trip — which is always a good thing. Where things get interesting is when the fishermen and the skunk start sharing the same territory along the shoreline at night.

**Raymond with a 15-pound bluefish that didn't get 'skunked.'**

I have written previously about the early fishing misfortunes of Raymond — after all, there were so many to choose from. In fact, during his early years of fishing, the name "Raymond" and getting skunked were synonymous. Nevertheless, leave it to Raymond to put a whole new twist on the phrase "getting skunked."

It was early October sometime during the mid-1980s. Raymond, Bruce, and I were fishing together one evening at the Point Judith Lighthouse. Before this fishing trip, Raymond had yet to catch his first keeper bass or a bluefish that weighed over 5 pounds. But on this night, Raymond had broken out of one of his curses and he had caught and landed a beautiful bluefish — a fish that would have easily tipped the scale at 15 pounds. He was ecstatic to say the least, dancing around up on the beach, shouting into the surf that his curse was gone and generally enjoying his newfound success. When he finally settled down, he dragged his prize bluefish high up on the rocky shoreline, where it would be saved for pictures and boasting later on (an activity that was heretofore foreign to Raymond's agenda). He then returned to the water's edge to begin casting once again. Now, like Jamestown, mainland Rhode Island has its share of skunks, and the Point Judith area was no exception. The skunks live in the brush and undergrowth near the shorelines and come out to the beaches during the night to forage for anything that the tides (or the humans) have left behind. In this case, a big fat bluefish must have looked like a giant turkey on Thanksgiving Day to the skunk that stumbled across Raymond's prize catch sitting up on the rocks. In fact, it wasn't long after Raymond had left his fish up there that Bruce noticed that something was moving around it and so he shouted over to Raymond to put his attention to it. As Raymond started to go up toward the fish, he suddenly realized that there was a skunk feasting upon his trophy and he stopped dead in his tracks. Perplexed for a moment on exactly how to remove this little pest without himself becoming a victim, he slowly backed away to a distance that he thought was out of the spray range and began to throw rocks at the varmint. It worked, and the skunk, begrudgingly, took off.

Unfortunately for Raymond, who was excited about having a "photo opportunity" with his fish, the damage had already been done. While we all had our backs turned as we were casting for more fish, the skunk had managed to eat the face off of both sides of Raymond's bluefish, transforming it from a prize catch into lobster-trap bait. When we arrived back at the house in Jamestown that evening, Raymond pulled the mutilated bluefish out of the truck and threw it up on the lawn, proclaiming, "This could only happen to me." Bruce and I were in hysterics. Hearing the laughter, Bruce's mother came outside to see what was going on. We told her that Raymond had achieved a new milestone — he was the only fisherman we had ever known to catch a fish and be skunked at the same time.

# Chapter X

## A Team Sport

It's always interesting to explore the history behind a sport, in particular how the sport began and how it evolved into its present-day practice and style. As with many sports, striped bass fishing enjoys a rich history, and a history that was influenced to a great extent by the culture of its participants, the fishermen, and by the patterns of fish as a species. There are plenty of accounts of striped bass fishing in New England that date back to the 1600s and 1700s and some even before that. It was well known then, as it is today, that the bass is a formidable game fish and excellent table fare.

During the 1800s, fishing for stripers became very popular among successful and wealthy businessmen. In fact, many fishing associations and clubs were established for the purpose of pursuing the striped bass, the most notable of which were the Cuttyhunk and Pasque Island clubs of the Elizabeth Islands. The Cuttyhunk Fishing Club was established in 1864 and the Pasque Club about 12 years after that. The membership list at each of these clubs reads like the Who's Who of American business in the late 1800s.

The methods these club members used to catch stripers wouldn't exactly stack up against the more sporting techniques employed by today's surfcasters, but the same enthusiasm for the sport seems to have prevailed. In those days, bass stands were erected for club members by driving parallel pairs of large iron rods into boulders protruding from the surf, some of these extending as far as 150 feet out over the water. Heavy wooden planks were then placed on top of the iron rod structure, forming makeshift jetties. A staff member of the club or a member's personal assistant would be hired to go down into the surf and chum with bait for the bass before the member started fishing, and the assistant would likewise have the responsibility of retrieving and gaffing any fish caught. All the while, the club member would be sitting in a comfortable chair atop the bass stand, fishing — with amber liquid in hand, no doubt. In those early years, plugs were not widely used, as bait-fishing was almost the exclusive protocol. And what would you suppose was the bait of choice for these fine gentlemen? Why, lobster, of course.

Block Island and Jamestown were not without their own fishing clubs and associations and you can still see the deteriorated and weathered remains of the islands' bass stands extending from the rocks in several places around the shorelines. One prominent Rhode Island lawyer and politician, Col.

Francis W. Miner, erected at least two bass stands on Block Island as well as a clubhouse on a bluff point that overlooked one of the stands. Miner had a reputation for catching very large bass and lots of them, but he stepped into the limelight when, during the summer of 1887, he reported that he had hooked and landed an 85-pound striped bass from the Block Island surf! It was big news, even then, and the story was reported in the papers along the entire East Coast. Unfortunately, the catch was never weighed in front of credible witnesses, or even photographed for that matter, which does lend a suspicious slant to the claim.

Like horse racing, rod-and-reel fishing for striped bass in the early years took on a sort of "sport of kings" status — at least as it was practiced and enjoyed by members of the exclusive bass clubs. The equipment, which consisted of long wooden or bamboo surf rods with wooden reels and linen line, was considered to be very specialized and generally not affordable for the average fisherman. That's not to say that stripers weren't pursued by all fishermen, because they most certainly were; but for the average guy, the standard method was a cotton hand-line with squid as bait.

The clubs also took great pride in providing the finest in creature comforts for their members, boasting extensive menus of exquisitely prepared beef, poultry, and, of course, striped bass. But just as the clubs had come into prominence, membership began to dwindle in the early 1900s due to an all-too-familiar problem — lack of resource. Similar to the decline of the mid-1970s and most of the 1980s, the bass population began a disastrous downturn during the late 1800s that continued through the 1920s. As a result, membership at the clubs and interest in rod-and-reel fishing for stripers diminished and many of the clubs closed their doors, including the prestigious Cuttyhunk Fishing Club.

The striper numbers started to make something of a rebound through the 1930s and 1940s. As the sport evolved, many fishermen who became experienced at catching bass for sport also discovered that it could be lucrative as well. The meat of the fish was in high demand and, since there were no limits on what a fisherman could take from the shore, many of the resident fishermen of Block Island, Jamestown, and the Cape supplemented their incomes with healthy catches of large stripers. Small groups of fishermen consisting of local residents on each island had formed their own impromptu fishing clubs and this time, in contrast to the clubs of the past, one of the objectives was to make money. Several groups of these men would follow the bass migration from Montauk to the Cape and back, fishing all night, selling their catch in the morning, and sleeping through the day — a tough routine, to say the least.

When the striper moratoriums and regulations were finally put into place in the 1980s, most commercial fishing for stripers by hook and line came to an abrupt end. Although it has taken many years of astute management and strict regulation, the striped bass fishery today is in better condition than at any time in recent history. The increase in bass numbers has also resulted in a resurgence of the sport and the creation, once again, of many new fishing clubs and associations. This time around, however, the emphasis is not on financial gain, nor on taking the fish in quantity — it is about the fishing challenge itself, conservation of the resource, and, of course, bragging rights.

Striper fishing can be both a team sport as well as an individual one-on-one competition between you and the fish. Some teams or clubs compete against each other and some compete only among their own members. Quite a few years ago, I founded what is now the Princeton Fishing Team — so called because the founding members (Bruce, Raymond, and I) are all originally from Princeton, New Jersey. It's not really a team and we don't compete with other clubs and, unlike the original Cuttyhunk Club, women *are* allowed and in fact constitute some of our most capable and determined anglers. There are about 20 members on our team; they have many different backgrounds and professions and live scattered across the country. The common thread, of course, is the love of a fine and challenging sport and a deep appreciation of the magnificent island fishing environments — an unspoiled environment that in today's world is becoming more of a rarity each year. Although it is often difficult for all of us to gather together at the same time, at least once each fall we rent one or two houses on the Block for a week and cross our fingers that the bass come in and the major storms stay away. I was not surprised to find out from one of the island's realtors that there are a number of fishing groups now doing the same thing. Fall fishing is sometimes the best fishing of the year and the rental rates at that time of the year are considerably less expensive than in the summer.

It's a definite departure from the way we did things many years ago, when we would sleep in our cars and rough it for many days at a time. Now, more than ever, it's the entire experience that's important, not just the fish. Getting together with great friends, in addition to the bass fishing, is what makes the experience complete and adds to some of life's finest memories. It's humorous as well to see how preferences change over the years. Whereas in the past, we would have been satisfied with beer, sandwiches and screw-cap wine, now the menu and spirit legend for our annual fall fishing trips rival that of the once exclusive Cuttyhunk Club.

**One of our team members, Debbie Donehey, with a nice spring striped bass.**

Several years ago while I was out on the Block on a spring fishing trip, a friend of mine had heard me talking about one of the houses where the group likes to stay in the fall and she asked if we could take a look at it. I said sure, but if there were renters in the house, I didn't want to impose. When we got there, we walked up onto the porch to look inside and when the folks inside saw us, two of the men came to the door. I explained to them that I had rented the house previously with the Princeton Fishing Team and that we had just come to admire it again. With a look of surprise, one of the men said, "Really?! Well, I'm the owner. Please come in, I'd like to show you something." I immediately thought to myself, "Uh-oh, what did we break?" He took us into the master bedroom, opened the closet door, and pointed to our pre-printed weekly menu, which included rack of venison, moose porterhouse steaks and, of course, fresh charcoal-grilled striped bass. The menu was still attached to the back of the door and before I could apologize for not removing it, he exclaimed with a huge grin, "I left this thing here on purpose — you guys are my inspiration! What an incredible menu; your group really does it right!" We all had a good laugh and after a brief tour of the house, my friend and I left to go back into town, but not before noticing that the owner, and the group that he was fishing with that week, had at least gotten one part of the menu correct — they had about four cases of excellent wine and several cases of other fine spirits sitting on the floor, ready for consumption. Now *that's* an inspiration.

**Princeton Fishing Team**
**2000 Fall Fishing Expedition**
**Crew Itinerary and Menu Schedule**

| 10/18<br>Saturday | 10/19<br>Sunday | 10/20<br>Monday | 10/21<br>Tuesday | 10/22<br>Wednesday | 10/23<br>Thursday | 10/24<br>Friday |
|---|---|---|---|---|---|---|
| Crew<br>Leo, Bruce<br>Raymond, Max<br>Debbie, Jim D<br>Harvey & Mike | Crew<br>Leo, Bruce<br>Raymond, Max<br>Debbie, Jim D<br>Harvey & Mike | Crew<br>Leo, Bruce<br>Raymond, Max<br>Debbie, Jim D | Crew<br>Leo, Bruce<br>Raymond, Max<br>Debbie, Jim D<br>Bill, Jim S. | Crew<br>Leo, Bruce<br>Raymond, Max<br>Debbie, Jim D<br>Bill, Jim S. | Crew<br>Leo, Bruce<br>Max<br>Debbie, Jim D | Crew<br>Leo, Bruce<br>Max<br>Debbie, Jim D |
| Menu<br>*6:00pm*<br>Charcoal grilled Black Angus Ribeye Steaks<br>Italian-style skillet potatoes with sweet red peppers and onions<br>Garden-fresh buttered green beans | Menu<br>*6:30pm*<br>Charcoal Grilled fresh Block Island Striped Bass (traditional style)<br>Wild Mushroom Sauté<br>&<br>Creamy whipped Yukon Gold potatoes | Menu<br>*6:30pm*<br>Linguini with a white wine garlic & basil sauce<br>Charcoal grilled Canadian Moose Porterhouse Steaks<br>Fresh Autumn garden salad | Menu<br>*7:00pm*<br>Dijon-crusted rack of venison in a wild-game reduction sauce<br>Grilled prosciutto-wrapped Atlantic prawns<br>Whipped potato garnish with grilled asparagus spears | Menu<br>*7:00pm*<br>Charcoal Grilled fresh Block Island Striped Bass (tarragon butter style)<br>Fresh green beans in mushroom-onion cream sauce<br>&<br>roasted new potatoes with shallots | Menu<br>*7:00pm*<br>Penne Rigate in a light northern Italian garlic & basil red sauce<br>Hearts of palm, tomato/basil salad in a balsamic vinaigrette | Menu<br>*7:00pm*<br>Fresh Block Islan Striped Bass (Emeril style)<br>Yukon Gold bake potatoes<br>Oriental stir-fry vegetables |
| Appetizer<br>Harvey's Boston Deli Assortment | Appetizer<br>Raymond's famous Clams Oreganatto | Appetizer<br>Orsi's Salmon Supreme | Appetizer<br>Traditional Tomato-garlic Bruschetta | Appetizer<br>Jim's Venison Chili | Appetizer<br>Bacon-wrapped Scallops | Appetizer<br>Budweiser<br>&<br>Amber liquid |
| High Tide<br>**2:09 pm**<br>SR 7:04 SS 6:02 | High Tide<br>**2:47 am**<br>**3:10 pm**<br>SR 7:05 SS 6:01 | High Tide<br>**3:45 am**<br>**4:07 pm**<br>SR 7:06 SS 5:59 | High Tide<br>**4:38 am**<br>**5:00 pm**<br>SR 7:07 SS 5:58 | High Tide<br>**5:27 am**<br>**5:48 pm**<br>SR 7:08 SS 5:56 | High Tide<br>**6:14 am**<br>**6:36 pm**<br>SR 7:09 SS 5:59 | High Tide<br>**7:00 am**<br>**7:22 pm**<br>SR 7:11 SS 5:5 |

10/18/2000 (D:\2003 fall menu1.doc)

Anyone who lives on or has rented on Block Island or Jamestown will be quick to tell you that the prices for real estate on both islands has gone through the roof — especially over the past five years, and especially on Block Island. There are a lot of descendants of the original island residents who never thought they'd be millionaires, but in fact, their homesteads and farmland are worth millions today. Personally, I think that's terrific. Many of these islanders have lived most, if not all of their lives in an environment that to the summer tourist, appears relatively warm and mild. In reality, the winters are long and brutally cold and the islands are frequently whipped by a merciless and constant north wind. You pay your dues when you live on an island and you suffer the additional inconvenience of having to cross the water to purchase major goods and services that for most of us are just a short drive away. I'm happy for the islanders who are now reaping the rewards of their many years of paying dues — and thankful to them for also keeping the islands in shape for the rest of us. My group has had the pleasure of renting and staying in many of the island homes. Our preferences, as you might guess, are dictated by the convenience of access to the prime fishing areas that we prefer to frequent, the availability of a well-stocked kitchen, and a working fireplace. Over the years, we have managed to establish quite a comprehensive system for getting everything out to the island in order to ensure pure fishing bliss, including firewood and a completely portable satellite television system — after all, you have to have news, sports, and weather. We take good care of the properties we rent, leaving them cleaner than when we arrived and in a better state of repair (two of our guys are retired engineers and they just can't seem to stop fixing things).

A lot of great fishing adventures and wonderful lifetime memories come out of these annual team fishing trips as well as some very funny stories; here are a few that are especially interesting and amusing…….

On one of our fall trips over to the Block, we rented a large and very beautiful waterfront home on Southwest Point. Quite a few of the regulars were supposed to come out for this trip, so we needed plenty of beds and a large kitchen, which this place had. It was the first week of November and the weather was quite mild for that time of year. Max, Bruce, Raymond, and I had arrived ahead of the others to set things up. My former business partner, Lou, was scheduled to fly in later that afternoon with one of our clients, Carl Stellwag, who had been invited out to fish with the team for a few days. Those of us already present had landed some very nice bass early that morning and, as was our usual custom, we put them on the floor in the outdoor shower for our arriving guests to inspect. I don't know how this custom got started, but the routine was to stack the bass in the shower stall, cover them with a wet towel, and close the door to keep the feral cats out. It was a very good way to keep the fish fresh for a while as long as the temperature outside was 55 degrees or less. Arriving guests were immediately pointed in the direction of the shower stall, knowing full well that they would have to endure some ribbing for arriving late.

Another routine on these outings is the tendency to overindulge in the spirit category upon first arrival. We've all learned through the years that when the cocktail glass is full, not much fishing gets done, so we try to keep that in mind — occasionally. However, I guess on the first day or night that you arrive on the island for an extended stay of fishing, the rigors of traveling (some of us fly thousands of miles to get there), coupled with the excitement and anticipation, is enough to merit an extra belt or two (the urge subsides after the first day as the focus is then directed more toward fishing). Lou and Carl arrived that evening, and following their tour of the outside shower, everyone settled in for cocktails and dinner. Not wanting to buck tradition, Carl fit in nicely with the rest of the group and after liberal amounts of amber liquid, he announced that he was too excited to wait for the morning and was going to walk down to Southwest Point and catch a bass.

Now Carl is one of the nicest guys you'll ever meet. He loves fishing and the outdoors, he has a great sense of humor, a heart of gold, and he's also a recipient of a Purple Heart. But he had never before fished for striped bass, he had never fished for striped bass *at night*, and he had no idea of what it was like to fish at Southwest Point. Fishing the Point at night is not for beginners. It requires standing (balancing yourself) on a field of very slippery, submerged rocks, while breakers come at you from three different directions. And after several cocktails, none of us except Carl wanted to go down to the Point and deal with that. Nevertheless, Carl was determined to do it and he put on his gear, which included a very nice Western-style fishing hat. Seeing that there was no stopping him, Lou figured that he had better escort Carl down to the Point and keep an eye on him lest we lose one of our best clients. So out the door they went with the rest of us laughing at them, but at the same time telling them to be careful as we went to settle in front of the fireplace.

No more than 20 minutes had passed when suddenly we heard a lot of banging around on the front deck of the house. The door opened and in walked Carl minus his favorite fishing hat, completely disheveled and as wet as a floor mop, but nonetheless laughing. Lou came in right behind him and of course the rest of us were all ears waiting to hear what happened. As Lou explained it, he had positioned Carl in a strategic spot down at the Point, cautioned him once again about the waves and the cross-currents, and then moved into a spot for himself that was just close enough to Carl so that he could see Carl's dark outline against the horizon. About two or three casts later, Lou looked down, and there, floating by him, was Carl's fishing hat. Seeing this, he turned to look back at Carl, but Carl's silhouette had disappeared. Lou figured he had better stop fishing and start looking for Carl, but he didn't have to look far. Carl was sitting on a log up on the shoreline after pulling himself out of the 55-degree water, in which he had taken an unscheduled and eye-opening bath. They both had a good laugh and decided to hang up the fishing until morning, when Carl would be able to see and understand a little more of what he had to deal with in the surf. After Carl dumped some of the Atlantic out of his waders and took a hot shower, Lou and Carl opened a bottle of vintage port to celebrate their safe return. No surprise that they never made it to fishing the next morning.

Not only did Carl arrive with a bang — he left with one too. It was a very nice trip that year, no huge bass were caught, but everyone caught fish and had a great time. By the afternoon of the last day of the trip, everyone except Carl, Lou, and I had already left. The house was clean and ready for the next renters, and all that was left for me to do was to pack up and shower. Lou and Carl were in the living room reading and waiting for me to finish so that we could all leave together. About halfway through my shower, there was a terrific noise that came from somewhere within the house — it didn't sound like an explosion, just a very loud crash. I knew this wasn't going to be good, but I decided that I would finish my shower before I went out to see what had happened. When I came out, Carl was standing in the dining room in front of the long wooden dinning room table. One look at his face and I knew that whatever happened was directly connected to him. I looked over at Lou, who immediately said, "I'm not saying anything." When I asked Carl what the incredible noise was, he said, "I didn't mean to do it." "Do what?" I asked. While I was in the shower, Carl had decided that if he could lie on his back on a hard surface, it might help to ease some of the soreness that was brought about by all the fishing. Seeing that the dinning room table was extra long, he climbed up on it and stretched out on his back. This worked out pretty well until he rolled to the side of the table where the leaf was sticking out with no leg support underneath. The table and Carl fell over sideways and when they both hit the floor, the antique cherry one-of-a-kind heirloom table split completely in two. Sixteen hundred dollars later, the Princeton Fishing Team owned some very expensive cherry firewood. Well, at least cherry wood is supposed to smell nice when it burns, right? Ever since then, we've tried to keep Carl away from tables and sharp objects.

Speaking of sharp objects..... With all the time spent near very sharp hooks — inside surf bags, hanging off the rods, and pulling them from the mouths of fish — you just know the inevitable is bound to happen. Sooner or later a hook is going to find its way into a place where it doesn't belong and where it's certainly not welcome. Almost all of us have had that misfortune at one time or another, including yours truly. Above the basement stairs at the Shepleys' house in Jamestown, for example, is a framed top-water plug with a large hook that has been cut in two. The caption underneath reads:

*"On this day of July 7, 1984, a 17-pound bluefish caught a 200-pound idiot with this plug."*

This was Bill Shepley's indoctrination into the hook-in-the-hand Hall of Fame. Lord knows I've had several entries into the Hall myself, not the least of which was accomplished while standing in the surf and bringing a plug-hooked striper too close to my waders, allowing it to catch me in the leg with the hooks of my own plug — thoroughly soaking the inside boot leg with seawater, which came in through the holes it made.

But the best "getting hooked" tale that I know comes from Max. Max will hate me for telling this story because he was truly embarrassed by it, but in reality, it could have happened to anyone.

Max was a former client of mine who retired quite a few years ago. I invited him out to fish with the team one year and he's become a great friend to all of us for life. Max was an orphan and a proud graduate of the Hershey School for Boys in Pennsylvania. He's had to fight for — and earn — everything he has in life and he's a great example of a self-made man. Max and I were fishing together one afternoon in October out at Black Rock. We were fishing a considerable distance apart that afternoon, barely within sight of each other. I had just climbed out onto a large rock and had begun to cast when I heard Max calling me over the radio. When I responded, he asked me how long I was going to be fishing from the spot that I had selected. I thought that might be a signal that he was ready to go, but since I had just climbed all the way out onto this rock, I told him that I'd probably fish there for another 10 or 15 minutes. He called back and said, "OK, well, I kinda have a little problem here, come over when you get finished." It turned out that Max had landed a 20-pound striper and, in the process of removing the plug, the fish had lunged to the side and sunk a treble hook into one of Max's fingers. Now if you don't already know, the last thing you want attached to a hook in your hand is a thrashing 20-pound bass on the other end. But Max had done the smart thing and had pinned the fish down on the beach with both of his knees. When he explained to me over the radio what the problem was, I told him to hold on and that I would be there right away. Max is such a considerate guy; only he would offer to wait for me to finish fishing my spot before calling me over to help with his situation. What he didn't tell me was that when he went to pin the fish down, the fish jerked to the side once again and now one of the front hooks on the plug had lodged into his *other* hand!

So there was Max, on both knees, pinning down a still-feisty 20-pound bass, attached to the fish by hooks that were stuck in both of his hands. We can laugh about it now, but I know he had to be just a *little* nervous at the time. Fortunately, Max had managed to get one of the hooks out before I got there. The other hook had penetrated his finger beyond the barb and was going to require some work. When I arrived, I unscrewed the treble hook that was still in his hand from the lure (removing the danger of the moving fish) and we headed back to the house — hook in hand. About 15 minutes after we arrived at the house, Max emerged from the bathroom with a smile on his face. And in place of the hook that was in his hand was a shot of whiskey. As I took a picture of him and his striper, I remember him saying in reference to the fish, "This was a tough one, but the bottom line is still: Max, one, fish zero."

**Max with the striper that hooked him almost as well as he hooked it.**

I can't say enough about how completely enjoyable these organized annual team trips are (the members of the Cuttyhunk Club were really onto something). One of my friends in Tampa once commented that it sure seemed like a lot of fuss to fly off to some island just to catch a bunch of fish. He was perplexed when I told him that sometimes we actually don't catch a "bunch" — we only catch a few, but we have a great time all the same. In fact, there are some years when the fall fishing on the islands just plain stinks. Successive ocean storms, very cold weather, or variations in the migratory patterns of baitfish can cause the majority of bass to bypass the islands, creating a very lean season.

When you can't fish every night of the fall season, you pick your fishing dates so that they correspond with good tides, little or no moon, and then cross your fingers. Such is life, but that still doesn't diminish the enjoyable aspect of getting out from behind the desk and into a magnificent island environment, and, for a few days at least, leaving your cares and problems behind you. I remember one year during the fall season when the wind blew at a constant 25 knots from the northwest for almost two weeks. I had never seen anything like it. I hate the northwest wind — it's a cold wind in the fall, and it's almost always a lean fishing wind. We caught very few stripers during our trip that year, and in fact, most of the guys left a few days early because of the wind conditions and the cold. Unfortunately for one of our newest members, Jim Donehey, it was his first trip out to the island. Jim was another former client of mine and is now a very good friend. He had heard me speak of all the great fishing experiences we had out on the Block and when he expressed interest, I invited him out. It was probably a good thing that most of the guys couldn't make the trip that year for one reason or another, and, as I mentioned, those who did left early.

Jim planned to fly in for the last three days of the trip even though I had warned him that the fishing up to that point had been very tough. Not having fished with Jim before, I wasn't sure he was going to be able to handle the fishing conditions he was flying into. In my experience, there are fishermen and there are *fishermen.* Fishermen will cast for a half an hour and if they don't catch anything, hang up the rod. *Fishermen*, on the other hand, will fish for hours on end and if they catch nothing, you still have to rip the rod out of their hands to make them stop. Jim is a *fisherman.* He and I pounded the island for three days, fishing through some of the toughest and most uncomfortable conditions that I had fished in a long time. Not one fish was caught between us. When we weren't fishing we worked on cleaning out the entire multi-bottle scotch supply (which took some doing) and solved all the world's problems in front of the fireplace. Did we have a great time? You bet.

**Bill Shepley, Jim Shepley, and the author with three small, but welcome bass on an October day when the temperature started out in the mid-20s during the early-morning fishing.**

ORVIS

# Chapter XI

## The Off-Season

At some point near the end of each year, we must put the rods, the waders, the plugs, and all the other equipment away for the winter. To me, that's always sort of a sad thing because it signifies the end of striper fishing for many months to follow. The interesting question, however, is when, exactly, do you hang it up for the year? For most striper fishermen, the end of the season is when, except for a few stragglers, the majority of bass have passed to the south to take up winter residence in the Chesapeake Bay or the Hudson River. The timing of this varies from season to season, but it usually happens around the end of October or early November. Are there exceptions? Most certainly. In fact, if you look back in striper history, you will find that during the so-called "glory years," the season frequently continued until sometime in December. And I'm not talking about the fish that over-winter in New England rivers such as the Thames River in Connecticut.

Twenty-five years ago, most of the die-hard striper fishermen knew that not only could the fall season extend well into December, but the majority of fish caught that late in the season would be big female cows. I guess I fall into the die-hard category because I rarely put the striper equipment away before December each year. In fact, it has become somewhat of a tradition for me to spend Thanksgiving out on the Block with family and/or friends celebrating the holiday, watching football, viewing the Macy's Thanksgiving Day Parade, eating turkey and, of course, fishing — although, curiously, over the past five years or so, the big bass haven't been around late in the November/December season as they used to be.

In recent years, depending upon the water temperature, there have almost always been fish present during Thanksgiving week on the Block, but they are invariably small schoolies, not the 40- and 50-pounders of the past. I wonder, though, if we might not begin to see the giant bass late in the season once again due to the simple fact that more and more very big bass are now starting to be caught throughout the regular season. Time will tell. My largest Thanksgiving striper was 31 pounds and was taken the day after Thanksgiving 2002. The latest I have ever caught bass from the Block was December 10, 1994 — when I caught two twin 25-pounders using the red-and-white Mirrolure and while most other folks were out Christmas shopping. One final note about late-season bass fishing: In my experience, once the water temperature of the surf permanently drops below 50 degrees, you can kiss the surf fishing goodbye for the season. I have never caught a striper from the surf in 40-degree water.

The onset of winter doesn't necessarily mean that all fishing has to come to an end. Many guys in New England hang up their striper rigs and break out the codfish equipment. I've never fished for cod from the surf, but those who have tell me that it can be a lonely, bone-chilling experience unless you do it from the inside of a beach buggy. In Florida, however, we don't have to resort to codfish; there's excellent inshore fishing to be had on the grass flats until the stripers are ready to return to their usual haunts again in the spring.

I'm frequently asked what "flats fishing" is. So for anyone who has never had the opportunity to experience inshore fishing in Florida, the term "flats fishing" refers to fishing the shallow saltwater grass flats in and around the mangrove shorelines along Florida's coastal regions. The primary species targeted (at least along the central west coast) are the sea trout, the redfish, and the snook, with an occasional tarpon and cobia thrown in for good measure. When I moved to Florida many years ago, I was concerned that my days of having excellent and challenging fishing would be limited to return trips to New England. I was delighted to discover that, quite to the contrary, Florida has some of the best year-round fishing in the country. And the fact that you *can* fish year-round is a bonus in the winter, when "striperitis" starts to set in. However, from mid-December to mid-February don't let anyone kid you — the fishing gets pretty slow along the central Gulf coast as well. It's not uncommon for water temperatures in the bays and along the Gulf shoreline to dip into the low 50s during that time of year, and while that might be fine for stripers, the trout and redfish bite will shut down, and for snook, prolonged exposure to temperatures in the 50s is life-threatening. By the middle of February, if the cold fronts are nice to us, the flats can come alive with all sorts of good fishing action and in water that's sometimes less than a foot deep.

One of the aspects of flats fishing that I really had trouble getting used to at first was the notion that there are some pretty big fish up in the shallow-water grass flats and they have nasty attitudes when stuck with a hook. The reason these game fish are found up on the flats becomes apparent once you've had an opportunity to take a close look at a mangrove shoreline. The mangroves are unique plants in that they actually live in the saltwater and their root systems form an extensive lattice-like network at the water line. This network of roots extends into the water and forms a perfect nursery environment for shrimp, baitfish, and juvenile game fish. It's no wonder then, that the bigger game fish are attracted to the mangroves as the dinner bell rings with every rising tide. And the big fish are particularly adept at swimming through root systems that are often encrusted with barnacles and oysters that will cut your line like a hot knife through soft butter. Snook are the specialists at doing this. When they're hooked, they'll head for the mangrove roots as if they have radar. It's one of the biggest challenges of snook fishing because the fish is often found right up against the mangroves — and trying to stop a 10-pound snook with 8-pound test line, well, you get the idea.

Another aspect of the flats that, for a striper fisherman, takes some getting used to is the tidal periods. New England's tides are pretty simple by comparison. In New England, if you take today's tide and add 45 minutes to it, you'll be fairly close to tomorrow's tide, and the tides occur at approximate six-hour intervals every day. Not so in the Gulf. On the flats, the tides are very irregular. You can have one-tide days or two-tide days — it's quite confusing and, for this reason, you have to keep an eye on the tide charts during the days you plan to fish. In such shallow water, it's easy to get caught with your boat in the flats back country on a receding tide, only to discover that you'll be spending the night because you don't have enough water to get back out.

Although you can fish the mangroves by wading, it's far more practical to do it from a boat that is specifically designed for the shallow flats. Actually, we do a little of both depending upon the season. In the winter, the water on the flats is often gin-clear and therefore the fish have an easy time seeing you standing in your boat while you cast at them. Generally, during the months of February, March, and April, we get out of the boat and wade-fish the flats. From late spring through the summer and into fall, the algae concentrations cloud the water and make it much easier to fish from a boat without being detected. The most wonderful thing about flats fishing is that it is remarkably similar in so many ways to fishing for striped bass with plugs. The environment is different to be sure, but the same basic methods that you would use to catch a bass or bluefish using a top-water popper in New England work equally as well on reds, trout, and snook. The southern division of the Princeton Fishing Team never uses bait; however, the majority of flats fishermen do. We probably catch fewer fish as a consequence, but we seem to catch a lot more of the bigger fish. Plus it's far more exciting than bait fishing. There's also no need for the 11-foot New England surf rods down here; a light 7-foot graphite spinning outfit with 8- or 10-pound test is perfect for fishing top-water artificials, which is primarily what we use. I can tell you that there's not much that compares with the feeling of excitement you experience each time a big snook smashes a top-water plug.

As the striper is the master and king of the New England surf, the snook is the master and king of the flats. The two fish are very similar in many ways, each being an incredibly powerful swimmer. Stripers grow larger than the common snook, which can reach a maximum size of around 50 pounds; however, the average size found on the flats these days is more in the range of 5 to 20 pounds. The snook is also excellent table fare and, like the striped bass, has delicious white meat and a very mild flavor. I actually prefer it slightly over bass, and I love the flavor of bass. It's interesting that for many years the snook was nicknamed the soapfish because when a snook fillet is cooked with the skin still attached, it gives the meat a soapy flavor, and it was generally not eaten for this reason. But once the skin is removed, the fish is perfectly delicious. One characteristic that distinguishes the snook from the striped bass is its propensity to jump when hooked. Stripers seldom jump out of the water, but a snook will leap completely out of the water many times, each time shaking its head rapidly back and forth, trying to throw the attached plug. And by the way, they're usually quite successful. When snook decide to go after a plug, it's electric — they don't hold anything back, it's all or nothing. They will crash the surface so hard it makes your heart skip a beat and it creates a commotion that would lead you to believe that a fish three times its size had attacked. The initial run is a screamer and if your drag is too tight when a snook strikes, you'll lose the fish because, in most cases, your line will snap before you have a chance to adjust it.

I have so many great snook stories; however, a striper chronicle is not the place to tell them. But recently someone reminded me of an interesting encounter that I had with a snook and the story is just too precious not to pass along here. I was fishing the grass flats a few years ago in early spring with a friend of mine and her 12-year-old daughter. As I mentioned before, just as in New England, my group never uses bait — only artificials. The only time that bait is ever allowed on my flats boat is to introduce young kids to fishing because it would be too much to expect a youngster to be able to handle the task of accurate casts with lures along the mangroves the first time out. It's better to let kids feel the excitement of the take and the catch (and the live release) before getting more complicated. So live shrimp were added to the bait well that morning as the selected bait of the day. The preferred method is to place a live shrimp under a flats bobber (which is conically shaped, with the bottom painted to match the color of the water) and to cast it into strategic places along the mangrove shoreline. Live shrimp are like candy to snook, reds, and trout, and that day the candy was in demand. By noon this young lady had boated 12 redfish and two nice trout — each fish gingerly released. Shortly after noon, we had changed spots because the redfish bite had turned off in the previous location (I think she caught all that were there). When we got ourselves anchored in the new spot, I made a cast toward the mangrove shoreline with a fresh shrimp and handed the young lady the rod. It wasn't but a few seconds before the bobber disappeared and line was peeling from the reel. Before I could say "snook!" the fish shot out of the water, shaking as if it were being electrocuted and then it did the same thing two more times. The third jump was too much for the line and it snapped, leaving the three of us gasping and asking each other, "Did you see that? Wow! Did you see that?" We marveled at the fish's aerial display and then reeled in the remaining line.

The line had apparently broken off ahead of the bobber, because everything from the bobber down was missing. Well, not for long. Out in the middle of the little cove, away from the mangroves, up popped the bobber – snook still attached and moving slowly forward. "There it is, there it is!" shouted the young lady. And right at that moment, an idea struck me. I told everyone to sit down, we were going after it. I pulled anchor and put the electric trolling motor on high. As our flats boat drew near, we saw that the bobber was up for a few seconds, then down for a few seconds. So I grabbed one of the rods that was rigged with a small sinking Mirrolure. I had no doubt that the snook wasn't about to let us close enough to grab the bobber, but if I could make a cast with the sinking Mirrolure and snag the leader between the snook and the bobber, well, we might have a chance. First cast, a miss. Second cast, another miss. Then the snook turned and ran right by the boat and the third cast managed to intercept the line right between the fish and the bobber as we all held our breath to see if the plug would catch the line and if the bobber would hold long enough to get the fish to the boat. Miraculously it did and we finally boated this snook, which we had to catch twice. It was not a huge fish after all; in fact, it was an inch under the minimum allowable size for a keeper. No matter – we were all just happy to have had the experience and to be able to free the fish from trailing a bobber around all over the flats, potentially endangering its life. It was a happy ending for all involved.

**Kristen Orsi with a keeper redfish (which she always released) caught on a top-water red-and-white Mirrolure.**

The redfish is the second most sought-after fish on the flats. Redfish are very similar in character and fighting style to bluefish — they are the bulldogs of the flats. Like bluefish, reds, when hooked, will fight and fight and fight until they completely exhaust themselves. Redfish can grow as large as striped bass, however, reds that big are rarely encountered on or near the Gulf coast flats. Like the snook, the average-size redfish found on the flats these days is between five and 20 pounds. Redfish will readily strike a top-water plug when it's presented correctly, although since a redfish's mouth is lower than that of most other fish, redfish tend to have difficulty taking surface plugs, sometimes striking several times before a hook-up. Another trait that separates reds from other fish on the flats is that a red will sometimes trail a top-water plug for several yards just before striking it. This will often create a large v-shaped wake behind the plug before the strike, making it no secret that you're just about to get slammed — it will make your heart pound! Similar in texture and taste to the striper, redfish fillets are delicious — after all, who hasn't heard of "blackened redfish"?

**Team member Ron Schneider with a beautiful redfish which was over the size slot limit (27") for a keeper and was therefore quickly released following a snapshot.**

Anyone who's ever caught a squetegue (or weakfish, as they're also called) from New England waters would find it easy to make the comparison between it and a Gulf coast sea trout — they appear almost identical. And actually, the fish are related; however, they are not the same fish. Like their New England cousins, sea trout are very aggressive, and even the young fish will strike a top-water plug that's half its size. Gulf coast sea trout don't grow to be as large as sea trout in the Atlantic, but as a result of the Florida commercial net ban and tighter restrictions on recreational take, we have started to see some very large fish being caught on the west coast. It used to be that a 24-inch Gulf coast trout was a lifetime trophy, but during the past two years, many trout between 24 and 30 inches have been reported. Trout will aggressively attack a variety of top-water lures and, when hooked, they characteristically thrash back and forth on the surface of the water in an exciting display before getting their bearings and heading deep to fight.

So what happens in the striper off-season? Well, in Florida, at least, there are three good reasons to keep fishing until the stripers come back — snook, redfish and trout.

When I first started fishing the Florida flats, I used an old aluminum canoe that I rigged with an electric trolling motor. I didn't get anywhere fast, but it made cruising over 10 inches of water a real snap. It also presented a low profile, which enabled a stealthy approach — and when fishing on the flats, that's very important. When big redfish are up on a shallow grass flat, it doesn't take much to spook them and make them bolt for deeper water. They always seem to be nervous about being in such shallow water anyway, but they go there because that's where the food is. Bumping the anchor on the side of the boat, dropping a beer can on the deck, or closing a hatch cover too hard will transmit sound immediately to the fish's sensitive lateral line and put it on alert that something's up.

One of the reasons the redfish's mouth is in a lower position compared to most fish is because it frequently feeds off the bottom. When it does this in relatively shallow water, nosing around in the grass and sand bottom, its tails will often protrude from the surface of the water in a show of what is commonly referred to as "tailing." There is nothing more enticing to a flats angler then coming up on a school of tailing redfish — it's an amazing sight and it looks as if the fish are waving and saying, "Here I am, come and get me." Unlike snook and trout, reds have a tendency to bunch up in large schools of 50 to 100 fish, and if the flat is quiet and there's no boat traffic, they will very often stay in the same location through an entire tide. I have been lucky enough on several occasions to encounter a school of feeding reds up on the flats, and each time it was nonstop catch-and-release action that made the old arms sore the next day (of course I received no sympathy from anyone about the soreness).

One of the benefits of fishing the flats in late winter and early spring is that there are very few thunderstorms, and with Tampa being known as the "lightning capital of the United States," that's a significant consideration.

People who fish the Florida flats take lightning very seriously — and those who don't aren't around to talk about it. By late spring and all through the summer, you're lucky if you can get a full day of fishing in without being chased off the water by a lightning storm. During that time of year, afternoon thunderstorms are almost a daily certainty. But during late winter and early spring, the temperatures are usually mild and lightning storms are rare. I remember one afternoon in July about 15 years ago. My former business partner Lou and I decided to leave the office early and head for the flats. We had heard reports that, a few days earlier, some nice schools of redfish had been sighted along one of the shorelines in lower Tampa Bay. The thunderstorm patterns that week were unusual in that the storms were occurring along the coast during the morning and then moving inland in the afternoon — it's usually the opposite. Since on that day the morning storms had already passed us, we figured that we were in pretty good shape, so off we went in the canoe, cruising the flats and looking for reds.

After several seasons on the flats, I had really turned the canoe into quite the fishing machine. It was outfitted with a 40-pound-thrust electric trolling motor, PVC rod racks front and rear, beer holders, of course, and a centrally located cooler. Using just one 12-volt deep-cycle marine battery, we could troll around the flats for the entire day, although we never ventured much farther than two or three miles in any one direction. I remember that afternoon that the sky was slightly gray and overcast with the cloud remnants of the storms that had passed earlier, but there was no rain, no lightning, and no thunder — we never gave the weather a second thought. I had motored in the canoe over the grass flats about a mile offshore (still in about 12 inches of water), searching for signs of redfish, either tailing or swirling. The reason the flats are often called "grass flats" is because the bottom is covered with turtle grass that grows about eight to 10 inches off the bay floor. The grass provides a living environment for shrimp, small fish, and all sorts of marine organisms — all dinner items for snook, redfish, and trout. As we cruised along that afternoon, I kept hearing a noise, but it was so slight that I didn't pay any attention to it at first. After a while, it became somewhat annoying and I looked around to see what it was. Every few seconds, there were little ticks that sounded as though they were coming from a lure or a tight line on one of the stowed rods slapping ever so slightly against the rod body. Since we were cruising at that point and not fishing, each of us had two fishing rods that were rigged with plugs and standing upright in their PVC rod holders. Finally, I couldn't stand the irritating noise any longer and I told Lou that I was going to stop the electric motor so that we could figure out where the noise was coming from. When the noise of the motor stopped, it didn't take long for both of us to realize that the noise was the sound of tiny sparks that were flying skyward from the tips of our rods. We were so positively charged with static electricity that it was snapping from the rods and into the atmosphere. This phenomenon, known as St. Elmo's Fire, is a clear indication that you are a prime target for a lightning bolt. Horrified, I glanced at the back of Lou's head only to notice the small, loose ends of his hair standing up, and then I saw that the hair on my arms was doing the same thing. I can laugh about the experience now, but at that point, there were two fishermen who suddenly realized that their boat had become a floating lightning rod. In a panic, we took the rods down and put them inside the canoe, broke out the paddles, *and* cranked the trolling motor to high for a very anxious one-mile ride back to shore that took only 10 minutes but felt like an hour. You've never in your life seen two guys so ready to stop fishing and so happy to reach the shore.

As a side note, there are quite a few people that are struck by lightning on the Gulf coast every year, and many are fatalities. Interestingly, it is usually not the fishermen who are struck, but the beachgoers who ignore the deadly potential of lightning and fry in their ignorance. With that said, New England has its share of thunderstorms as well and an 11-foot surf stick makes a hell of a lightning rod — but I guarantee you, I'm not going to be the one to test how well it works.

On the Gulf coast flats, as with the surf in New England, you never know what might venture up into the shallows for a meal. Many years ago, I was fishing from the canoe in March in a spot that had consistently produced good catches of large trout. In fact, I had won several local tournaments with sea trout from this area and in so doing thoroughly miffed a lot of the guides who couldn't figure out how this "striper guy" was beating them at their own game, and without bait! One of the techniques I have found to be very effective is to start upwind with the canoe and drift over the flat, spraying casts with a plug in all directions, but always with the wind. When I would find evidence of fish, I would immediately anchor and fish the vicinity more thoroughly. And so it was that morning. I had the anchor down and had taken a few big beautiful trout when, all of sudden, I had a monster fish smash my top-water plug and take off for Mexico. I remember thinking; *Omygod, this is the biggest trout I have ever had on.*

I was sure it was a trout because in many years of fishing this spot I had never caught a snook or a redfish there; for some reason, the snook and reds never came up on this flat. I quickly realized that if I had any hope of boating this fish, I had better get the anchor up and the trolling motor on, because with 8-pound test and a little Penn 430, this fish was going to strip my reel unless I chased it with the canoe. So, back and forth across the flat I went with this fish, chasing it, getting it to within 15 or 20 yards of the canoe, only to have it bolt away each time on another long run. This fish wasn't fighting like a trout — trout don't possess that kind of stamina. It couldn't be a snook; it didn't jump. And it was way too fast to be a redfish. About 15 minutes had passed in the battle and by this time, I had the attention of several other fishermen who were on this flat and were now watching intently as the fish zigzagged across the water, with me in hot pursuit. Finally I started to gain on the fish as I was able to take in more line and its runs became shorter. The fish was now about 10 yards away, but it had found one of the deeper holes on the flat and was staying deep within it so I still couldn't see what it was. When I finally managed to get over the fish with the canoe and ever so slowly lift it from the bottom, I could not believe what I saw come to the surface. It was a 10-pound bluefish! Big bluefish are very rare on the flats, but I remembered hearing reports from other fishermen that during the winter months, very occasionally, bluefish would show up on the flats and surprise the hell out of an unsuspecting fisherman. It did, and I was.

There are many great fishing experiences on the Florida flats that I could write about, but as I mentioned earlier, the chronicles of striped bass adventures is not the place to tell them. However, with that said, there is one more story from the flats that I promised myself I would someday write about because it's almost too funny for words. It happened during the striper "off-season" when I was fishing with Lou and my Florida fishing buddy, Richard Michalski. The three of us were drifting the shallow grass flats, casting top-water plugs for sea trout on a mid-March morning. Now, three guys casting plugs in a decent-sized boat is tight, but this boat was an old 16-foot freshwater bass boat that we had converted for saltwater flats fishing and it made for very cramped quarters. Nonetheless, we had devised a casting system where each guy would cast to one area in front of him, or to the side, as the case may be, as we drifted forward with the wind at our backs — and it worked nicely. Even so, because of the space constraints, you really had to look behind you each time you swung your rod back in preparation to make a forward cast, just to make sure the plug, having three sets of trebles on it, didn't take someone's ear along with it. Well, for some reason this is a tough habit to get into for freshwater bass fishermen. Guys who have fished a lot for freshwater bass seem to instinctively take the rod and plug directly back over their head without looking behind them before launching a forward cast with a snapping, whiplike motion. Lou was one such fisherman. After hearing lures zip past our heads at less-than-comfortable distances that morning, Richard and I cautioned Lou repeatedly to look behind him before he cast. Lou would reply; "Don't worry, don't worry. I'm not gonna snag you guys — I know exactly what I'm doing." Less than convinced, Richard and I continued to lean in the opposite direction whenever one of Lou's backswings looked as if it was coming perilously close to flesh.

As we drifted along, picking up a trout here and there, I was standing and casting from the stern of the boat, Richard was standing and casting from the bow, and Lou was casting from the middle position. Since Richard and I were casting from either end of the boat, our tendency was to look out at the water in those directions with just an occasional glance back to the middle of the boat to keep Lou's backswings in check. Suddenly, just slightly out of the corner of my eye, I saw Lou take his rod back over his head to cast when there occurred a loud, sharp clacking sound from within the boat, immediately followed by a huge splash in the water in front of us. Richard and I turned at once to see what had happened only to find Lou with a startled look on his face. As unbelievable as it may seem, with his backwards over-the-head-without-looking motion, Lou had hooked one of his own spare rods that was lying in the boat behind him and then, in one continuous, forceful forward motion, he somehow managed to cast the hooked rod over his head, out of the boat, and into the water in front of us! As soon as Richard and I figured out what had happened, we were in hysterics for the rest of the day. The sight of the "master back-caster" reeling in his own fishing rod was too funny for words.

Finally, if you're not somewhere where you can fish during the striper "off-season," there are still plenty of organized activities available to help ease the pain until the linesiders return in the spring. Perhaps some of the best of these are sponsored individually by the local chapters of the Coastal Conservation Association (the CCA — now established in most states along the eastern seaboard) and the Rhode Island Saltwater Anglers Association (RISAA), a local state organization comprising over 3,500 fishermen.

Approximately 20 years ago, an organization of Florida recreational fishermen banded together to form the Florida Conservation Association (the FCA). The purpose of this nonprofit group was to build awareness of the need for managing the state's marine resources and coastal environment. It roughly coincided with the time that blackened redfish became a wildly popular dish and, as a consequence, the redfish stocks were being decimated. The FCA membership grew with the popularity of flats fishing, and the organization quickly became a strong voice that legislators needed to listen to. One of the group's first legislative accomplishments was giving redfish "gamefish" status. This not only ended commercial harvest of reds in Florida, but placed slot limits on keeper fish (18 to 27 inches) and initiated a one-fish-per-person daily limit. What was an almost devastated redfish Florida redfish population is now back to healthy proportions. And by the way, you can still have blackened redfish — you just have to catch one first.

The FCA was of paramount importance to the second and perhaps the biggest piece of Florida marine resource protection legislation — the net ban. In simple terms, a small number of commercial net boats had become so proficient at taking fish with their gill nets from the shallow flats that the resource was being destroyed quickly — and right in front of our eyes. Since a lot of the legislators were too sheepish to deal with the problem (probably because of accepting money from the commercial fishing industry lobbyists), the people of the state did it themselves by collecting enough signatures to force the placement of the amendment on the ballot as a change to the state's constitution. The amendment was approved by an overwhelming majority of 72% of the voters. So now when you shake off the ice and snow and come to fish these wonderfully productive grass flats that surround the Sunshine State, you can thank, in part, the members of this great group.

The same type of organizations had also been successfully formed in several of the other Gulf States, most notably Texas. Realizing that there is strength in numbers and much to be gained from sharing information and resources, the organizations have now combined into a single entity, the national CCA, with local state chapters. You may already be a member of your local CCA chapter or the RISAA, but if you're not, there's no excuse for not joining. The measly membership fees will help sustain a great organization whose primary purpose is to protect marine resources, including the striped bass. At least once a year, each chapter holds a major fund-raising event, which includes a multitude of fishing equipment, sportswear, trips, and even boats and motors up for bid at silent and live auctions. It's loads of fun and a good opportunity to catch up on the latest techniques and equipment, as well as to compare notes with other fishermen on the past season's successes.

# Chapter XII

## Equipment

I promised that this would not be a "how to" book. But since I'm frequently asked about my equipment preferences, I will describe some of the equipment and methods that have worked well for me over the past few decades. Keep in mind, however, that what works or feels comfortable for me may not be a good choice for you. There are a lot of options out there these days. Fishermen are inundated with advertising and catalogs from tackle companies pitching everything from fishing line to battery-heated socks. If you want to know what's killing our forests, you don't need to look much further than your own mailbox. I know I must receive a dozen or more catalogs every year from Orvis, L.L. Bean, Bass Pro Shops and Cabela's. I think it works out to three per company per season; the "master" fall catalog arrives at the beginning of the summer, the "fall clearance" edition arrives at the end of summer, followed shortly by the new "master" winter edition, and so it continues throughout the year. As much as it's overkill, it's also a real convenience if you pretty much know what you're looking for. I much prefer to shop for equipment from a catalog or online rather than having to make the trek to the store only to find out that the item you're after is out of stock. On the other hand, and for me at least, there are some things that are more difficult to purchase by catalog, particularly a fishing rod. I have to feel a fishing rod in my hands to be able to determine if the weight, balance, and action are exactly what I'm looking for.

Most of my early fishing equipment was inherited from my father. He fished with a 10-foot fiberglass surf rod that was thick enough to haul in a cow — a real cow. His reel was a conventional Penn Senator equipped with 50-pound test nylon braided line and his method was always to fish bait on the bottom. The rod bit the dust after several years in my possession because it was severed in two by the rear electric window of my station wagon — as I mentioned before, the early years had some trying moments. In search of a new outfit, I purchased an 11-foot white Penn Slammer that was made of graphite composite (whatever that was) and it was specifically designed and constructed for surfcasting with a spinning reel. It was a very good fishing rod at the time and it held up well through thousands of casts while being continuously subjected to a punishing marine environment. I was one of the only fishermen around Jamestown and Block Island to use this type of rod for many years, and when I pick up the rod today, I understand why. For all its qualities of endurance, the composite was very heavy in comparison with the all-graphite rods that are the current standard for surfcasters. I remember when I first switched over to an all-graphite rod. The rod was incredibly light in contrast to the telephone pole that I had been using, and I felt sure that I would snap it with the first cast. It took quite a few casts for me to finally realize that this surf stick, which was as light as a feather, could take everything I could give it and more. In fact, my casting shoulder is still in one piece thanks to graphite. The surf rods I use today are custom-made in Tampa by a friend and expert fisherman, Rick Redd. Rick has been building custom surf, flats, and fly rods for most of his life. About 10 years ago, we put our heads together to come up with a design for a surf rod that would take the punishment and the salt, provide for maximum casting distance, and have minimum weight and enough backbone to cast big plugs and fight 50-pound bass (well, you can always hope, right?). The resulting rod uses an 11-foot St. Croix two-piece graphite blank with reinforced stainless steel guides that are not chromed (the first and most important guide being at least 72 millimeters, outside diameter). It turned out to be a fabulous rod design — I can't say enough about it and my shoulder loves it endlessly.

My choice in spinning reels? That's easy — Penn, Penn, and Penn. I think there are more different kinds of reels available today than there are different kinds of cars on the road. The choices are amazing. Many years ago, I was investigating the possibility of starting a high-end fishing equipment company that would sell such merchandise through catalogs. Along with some of the other guys on the team, I field-tested a lot of the big-name spinning reel models. The unanimous conclusion was that, for the money, there was no better value than that found with the Penn line. Until about 10 years ago, I had exclusively used the Penn 704 model for so long that I can't remember when I started fishing with it. There are still a few in our stockpile that are over 30 years old, when they used to be gray or green — we don't use them anymore, but we could. And that's pretty much the point (you've heard the term 'bulletproof'?). The Penn 704 reels take abuse better than any other reels in the same price range and they keep on going. For many years, you could walk around Block Island in the fall and rarely see another type of reel on a surf rod. About 10 years ago, Penn introduced a skirted spool 650SS series for surf casting (now the 6500SS series) that in my opinion is its best model yet. The high-profile spool produces less resistance as the line departs, and the reel is lighter and more streamlined than the 704. The 6500 is as rugged as its 704 predecessor and still has the same great drag system. It's my choice, hands down.

As with reels, there's a plethora of choices in fishing line, with most brands claiming to have special scientific manufacturing processes or secret polymers that make their line better than the others. In my early years of fishing the surf, I couldn't discern any significant differences between the major brands of monofilament line; I just changed the line on the reels often enough to ensure that it maintained its strength and flexibility. When I began to fish more regularly, I noticed that some brands of line didn't hold up to the salt exposure as well as others, and in some cases, some brands of line even began to take on a dusty or faded appearance. After trying many different varieties through a long stretch of fishing seasons, I found that the line that seems to consistently hold its own over the others is Berkley Big Game. It's available in a green tint that becomes practically invisible underwater. I have pulled more big bass than I can remember around and over rocks in the surf with this line; it has excellent abrasion resistance and wears exceptionally well. Most surfcasters agree that if you use less than 20-pound test, you're asking for trouble if you get into a big fish. If you increase the strength, the next step up from 20-pound test is 25-pound test and while it's certainly stronger, it significantly reduces casting distance. Berkley Big Game, 20-pound test, green tint — that's my choice, at least.

As far as the microfilament braided lines go, the jury's still out on these lines for spinning reels. To be sure, they're far stronger and they last considerably longer then the finest monofilament available. This type of line is also very much smaller in diameter compared to the same strength of mono and as a result it allows for greater casting distances. For conventional reels, it's probably the way to go these days. For spinning reels, the line is so thin that it will cut into your casting finger in just a few casts — you simply must use a finger protector, which I don't like to do. The thinness of the line also gives it a tendency to dig into itself on the winds of the spool, causing knots that are practically impossible to remove without a needle and a magnifying glass (not something you want to be doing in the middle of the night and when the bass are hitting). Finally, if your drag isn't perfectly set, the no-stretch properties of the line make it much easier for a big fish to rip a plug from its mouth with a jerk of its head, whereas with mono the extra "give" in the line makes this much more difficult for a fish to do. Food for thought.

I'm not going to discuss rigging, leaders, and knots since the "how to" books do a thorough job on that subject; however, suffice it to say that you must always use a leader (mine is usually 50-pound test and a minimum 30-inch length), especially when fishing the rocky shorelines of Block Island and Jamestown. One other thought on this subject: I never use terminal tackle, like a snap swivel, to attach a plug to the leader. I don't know if the bass can detect them — some of the experts swear they can — so why take the chance? I use an "improved clinch" knot to tie the lures directly to the leader and the knot has failed me only once in 30 years — and that's because I tied it wrong.

So which plug works best? I wish I knew because I'd use it all the time and dump the other several hundred plugs I own. But no matter whom you ask, there always seems to be some variation in personal preference. It is often said that much of the lure design process is directed at catching the fishermen, not the fish, and most of our tackle boxes are testaments to that. Just about every surfcaster I know has a ton of lures in his or her tackle box, most of which are seldom used. Nevertheless, all are carted around on each fishing excursion "just in case." The tendency is to get comfortable with one or two plugs that have proven successful and then leave the others for when things get really bad, the rationale being that if the fish didn't want this plug, maybe they'll want that one, or this one.... then again, maybe the fish aren't there? Hello?! We fishermen are a funny bunch sometimes.

I have always been convinced that, on any given day, just about any plug presented properly under a striper's nose will have a good chance of drawing a strike. The main requirement, of course, is that the fish are, in fact, there. So without getting into a debate over which plugs work the best, I'll simply tell you which have been the standouts in my 30 years of throwing them into the surf. For stripers, in my opinion, there is no better plug than a swimmer — day or night, it doesn't matter. At the top of my swimmer list is the Mirrolure model 103 (red head, white body). Too many times for it to have been coincidental, I have stood on the shoreline with four or five other guys and outfished every one of them with a Mirrolure. The 103 is a floating plug that will swim just underneath the surface of the water with a slow retrieve. To achieve the perfect depth and action, we have found that it is necessary to reduce the plastic lip on the lure by about half using a sharp knife or, better yet, a grinder. The resulting action is a slow, injured-type swimming motion similar to that of the Danny swimming plug. Running close seconds to the Mirrolure are the Rebel and the Redfin. These swimmers are also similar in body style to the Mirrolure and they too have plastic lips that make them swim under the surface. Completing my selection are the needlefish, the Danny, and the Atom Junior blue-and-white swimmer. Color? Well, on this issue, the statement I've heard repeated by so many of the old-timers is, "Any color's fine as long as it's red and white." Do I believe it? Not really. Do I in fact fish with a red-and-white Mirrolure most of the time? Yes.

Actually, a lot of things in the ocean like the Mirrolure. One year, I received a call at my office from Harvey Waxman about midweek after he had been out fishing the Block one summer weekend. He said that I should sit down because he had a very big fish story to tell me. I thought to myself, "Oh hell, I'm going to have to hear about some 50- or 60-pound bass that he's landed and then I'll have to cry in my beer for the next week." Well, not exactly. While Harvey was fishing from Southwest Point one night that weekend, he had a nice hit about halfway in on his retrieve. Because it was summer, he was standing about waist-deep in the surf, without waders, and casting with one of the Mirrolures I had given him. The fish put up a tremendously long fight, and after about 15 minutes had passed, Harvey was thinking that this was surely the biggest bass that he'd ever caught in his life. He explained to me that as the fish finally started to tire and get closer to him, its dorsal fin surfaced about 10 yards from where he was standing. Much to Harvey's shock and amazement, it wasn't a striper's dorsal fin — it was a huge shark. The shark had taken the Mirrolure and headed for Montauk until Harvey interrupted its course by almost pulling it up alongside of him.

Fortunately, he was able to back out of the water and then beach the shark, which turned out to be a mako of well over 100 pounds. I never did hear how they got the plug away from the shark that night, but I understand that once it had relinquished Harvey's plug, the shark was returned to the water with the use of some logs that were on the beach. I doubt that Harvey did much casting from *in* the water during the rest of his stay that weekend.

As far as what plugs are best to use at what times and in what situations, well, there have been volumes written about this subject in the "how to" books and I'll just leave it at that. However, I will mention that I'm not in the camp of the dark-night/dark-plug, light-night/light-plug theory. It's never worked that way for me and, in fact, I've found that it works to your benefit to do just the opposite — and if you think about it, that's what makes the most sense anyway. Why would you want to throw a dark plug into a dark ocean on a completely dark night? So that the bass can see it better? I don't think so. On the other hand, it doesn't take rocket science to figure out that a dark plug contrasts beautifully against a light, moonlit surface. No matter which plug you select to take that 50-pounder, there's one thing that you should always do to increase your chances of getting it to shore — and that is to change out the standard-issue hooks with laser-sharp 4X-strong replacements. I only wish that I could have all the bass back that I've lost to bent hooks. Unless your lures come standard with 4X-strong hooks, and I don't know of very many that do, invest in replacements — you'll be glad you did. My preference is the Owner 4X-strong "ST" (for super tinned) trebles. I have never found a treble hook that could match their strength, sharpness, and anti-corrosion properties. It's as simple as that.

Block Island is one of the most punishing environments on earth for chest waders, and if you're going to fish the spring and fall seasons, you must wear waders because you *will* get wet. Climbing over barnacle-encrusted rocks and walking great distances over the island's boulder fields seems to significantly shorten the normal lifespan of even the best waders. For that reason, investing in the best chest waders that money can buy may not be a very good idea for fishing the Block. Two considerations that *are* important involve comfort. Fishing the spring or fall seasons can fluctuate between summer-like and brutally cold conditions. As a consequence, most of the surfcasters I know now have at least two pairs of chest waders, one set of neoprenes and one set of breathables. Chest waders are made in two different styles — stocking foot and boot foot. The stocking-foot variety requires that you buy a separate pair of boots to slip on over the wader's stocking foot. This type of wader system is used more for freshwater stream fishing and is completely impractical, even dangerous, for fishing Jamestown and the Block. A moderately priced pair of neoprene chest waders of 3 mm thickness, with knee pads and an internal chest pocket, has worked very well for me, even on the coldest Thanksgiving nights when the air temperature has been in the low 20s. I am told that soon to be available will be neoprene chest waders with a waterproof fly zipper, and what a tremendous improvement that will be. I can't even count the number of times I have dreaded having to take off all the gear just to get rid of a little beer. This type of wader is currently available only in duck hunter camouflage, which looks a little ridiculous on the surf fishing scene, but when they manufacture them in plain colors, they'll be a big hit with the surf fishing crowd.

Aside from the basics, technology has given the surf fishermen a few pieces of equipment that in recent years have really helped to improve the surf fishing experience and the safety of the sport. Three such items are the hand-held radio, the $CO_2$ inflatable vest, and the nightvision scope. I have mentioned previously that most of our team members now carry small waterproof hand-held radios for communication with other people in the group. They really come in handy for exchanging information, but also add an element of safety if someone gets into trouble or is injured. The radios allow you to set transmission frequencies to your own code, letting you keep your discussions about the huge bass you're catching (or wishing for) between you and other members only. Wearing an inflatable vest is just plain good common sense if you climb out onto the rocks as far as I do. There are several places on the Block and a few on Jamestown where if you fell in with chest waders on, you might have seen your last day of fishing. The $CO_2$ inflatable vests that are available from most of the major catalog companies are so small that you don't even realize you're wearing one. It's about 2 inches wide and hangs flat around your neck, and for less than $100, it might turn out to be the best piece of fishing equipment you ever bought. A night vision scope is more of an expensive toy than a necessity. I purchased one several years ago to help navigate my way through the mangrove islands of the Florida grass flats at night. Since the scope is also completely waterproof, it allows you to see how many other guys are fishing a particular area at night so you don't take a mile-long walk down the shoreline boulder field only to find a crowd already fishing at your intended destination.

Speaking of intended destinations, it often happens that one fisherman will comment about how he was fishing in a cove on a particular night and really got into the fish, while three other guys might have visited the same cove on the same night and not had so much as a bump. This is not uncommon. It happens because fishing the Jamestown and Block Island coastlines is very much different than fishing a straight flat beach. Just as the Cape has its bars, rips, and eddies, so too do the islands have their special nooks, indentations, and irregularities. It is often these subtle structures in the coastline that make the difference between fish and no fish.

I could send someone to fish Beavertail on Jamestown, for instance, telling him that it was a great spot for big stripers in the fall (which it is). However, without knowing the intricacies of the rocky, cliff-like shoreline, that fisherman might have to spend many days of fishing before tying into a nice fish. Any way you look at it, it's never a bad idea to improve your luck by conducting a little investigation of the shoreline during fishing's "off hours." For many years I've studied the coastlines of Jamestown and the Block by visiting the shore during the day and during periods of extreme low tide, even taking pictures for future reference. An astute fisherman can gain a lot of insight as to where one might reasonably predict fish to frequent at high water by studying the bottom's contour and the positioning of major rock formations in this fashion. It takes lots of observation and persistence, but it pays off.

Finally, no level of experience, no piece of equipment, and no special advice can ever take the place of plain old good luck — the one element in fishing you can't buy. And would I rather be lucky than good? Well, to borrow a phrase from the late Norman Daignault, "You bet!"

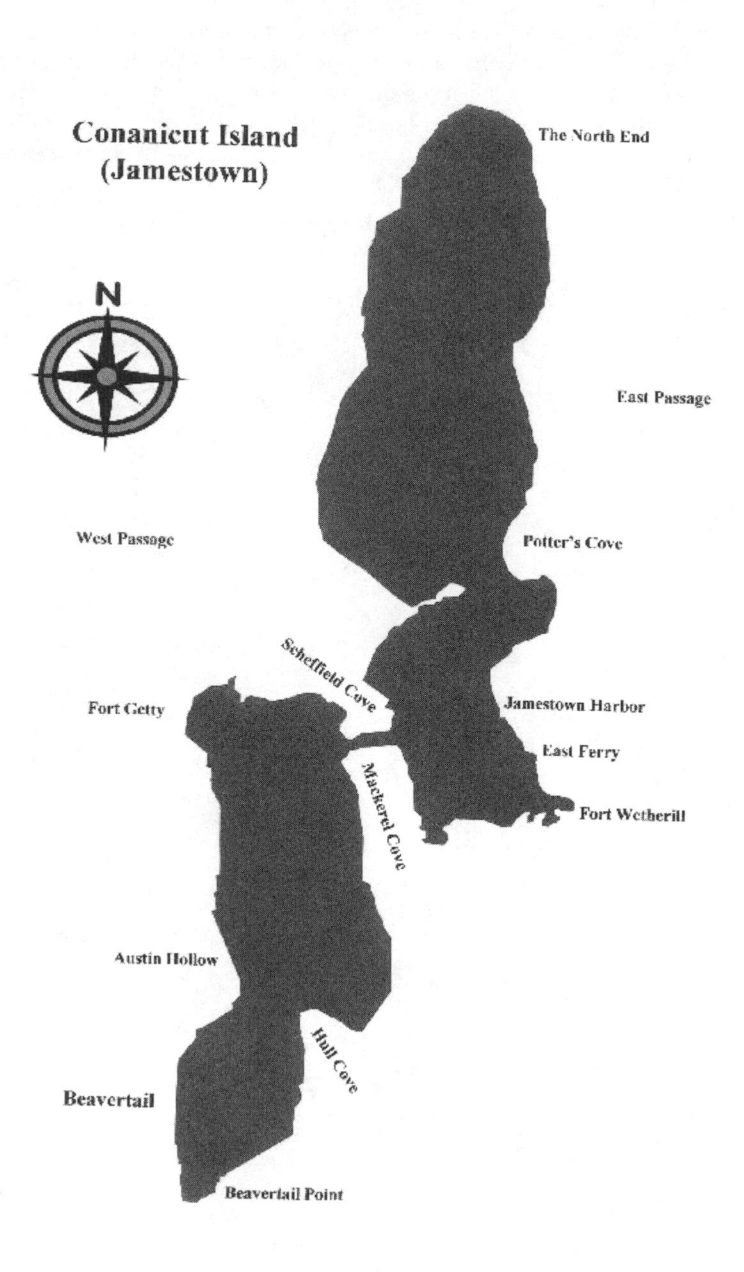
Conanicut Island
(Jamestown)
N
The North End
East Passage
West Passage
Potter's Cove
Scheffield Cove
Fort Getty
Jamestown Harbor
East Ferry
Mackerel Cove
Fort Wetherill
Austin Hollow
Hull Cove
Beavertail
Beavertail Point

# Epilogue

So there you have it — over 30 years in the suds and still relentlessly going back into the surf for more fishing excitement, season after season. Is it the lore and enticement of someday catching that 50- or 60-pound bass that keeps me coming back? Yes. Is it an appreciation for the unique character and beauty of the islands? Yes, without question. And the solitude offered by the nighttime coastline under starlit skies — a peaceful solitude, ever more difficult to find in today's world — could it be that also? Yes again. But above all, the most compelling, the most magnetic, and the most endearing aspects of this great sport that constantly beckon the soul to return to the surf time and time again are the chronicles — chronicles of exciting fishing adventures and memories that I have been so fortunate to share with, and that would never have been possible without, one of life's greatest assets — a remarkable group of extraordinary friends. Tight lines to all.